Tamaki Nozomu Presents Dance In The Vampire Bund 3

ダンス イン ザ ヴァンパイアバンド

3

環 望

On nous réconcilia:

Nous nous embrassâmes,

et depuis ce temps-là nous sommes ennemis mortels.

We reconciled

and we embraced.

And since then,

we have been mortal enemies——

Alain René Lesage, Le Diable boiteux

Dance In The Vampire Bund 3

Contents

Chapter 13: A Solemn Promise
3

Chapter 14: Moving Shadows
33

Chapter 15: Children of the Night
63

Chapter 16: Werewolf ~Beowulf~
95

Chapter 17: Strategic Chess Game
131

Chapter 18: Sacrifice
163

Chapter 19: Body & Mind
199

Appendix: Dance in the Vampire Maid
232

Tamaki Nozomu Presents Dance In The Vampire Bund 3

IT WAS THAT NIGHT...
WHILE STANDING THERE, UNDER THE PALE MOONLIGHT...
WHEN I KNEW IT...
THAT MY LOVE WAS OVER...

Chapter 13: A Solemn Promise

YUKI-CHAN!
OH, TOMO-SEMPAI!
HEY, I HAVEN'T SEEN YOU AT ALL LATELY!
I KNOW YOU'VE BEEN REALLY BUSY WITH THE STUDENT COUNCIL...
BUT *TRY* TO COME TO CLUB SOME-TIMES, OKAY?
WE ALL ENJOY READING YOUR WORK.

UM, WELL...
I HAVEN'T FELT LIKE SITTING DOWN AND WRITING ANYTHING LATELY...

AW, REALLY? WELL, THINGS HAVE BEEN ROUGH AT SCHOOL.

JUST KEEP ON SMILING AND IT'LL ALL WORK OUT!
AND REMEMBER, YOUR FANS ARE WAITING!
I WILL!

IT'S BEEN TWO WEEKS SINCE THE EVENTS IN THE CHAPEL.
EVERYTHING'S BACK TO NORMAL AT SCHOOL...
IF YOU DON'T LOOK TOO CLOSELY.
KEEP OUT KEEP OUT KEEP OUT
KEEP OUT KEEP OUT KEEP OUT

YES, THERE'S STILL A LOT OF REBUILDING LEFT TO DO.

KNOCK
KNOCK

EXCUSE ME.
CREAK

YES.
YES, OF COURSE.

NO, THIS TIME WE WERE IN THE WRONG AS WELL.
WE CAN'T HELP IT IF PEOPLE SLANDER US BECAUSE OF IT.

NO, YOUR HIGHNESS. DON'T WORRY ABOUT IT.
IT'LL BE GOOD MEDICINE FOR MIZOGUCHI-KUN.
IT WAS HIS FLAIR FOR THE DRAMATIC THAT MADE THINGS TURN OUT THIS WAY.
SINCE WE'VE ALREADY RECEIVED PAYMENT, WE HAVE AN OBLIGATION TO UPHOLD THE DEAL.
EVEN THOUGH HE *IS* THE MINISTER IN CHARGE OF THE SPECIAL DISTRICT, HE HAD **NO** RIGHT TO INTERFERE.

DON'T WORRY. NO ONE IN THE CURRENT GOVERNMENT HAS TAKEN IT AS A THREAT AGAINST JAPAN.
EVEN IF THEY HAD, MY PARTY WOULD HAVE TAKEN RESPONSIBILITY AND SETTLED IT.

IF ISURUGI-DONO WISHES TO, WE CAN MEET IN PERSON.
I'M VERY SORRY TO HAVE CON-CERNED YOU.
WHAT ARE YOU TALKING ABOUT? IT'S NOT AN OVERSTATEMENT TO SAY THAT OUR COUNTRY'S **FUTURE** IS ONE WITH THAT OF THE SPECIAL DISTRICT.
SO I LOOK FORWARD TO DEALING WITH YOU IN THE FUTURE.

PLEASE STOP BY MY HOUSE SOON.
I HAVE SOME *WONDERFUL* YOSHINO CHERRY TREES. THEY LOOK LOVELY AT NIGHT, AS WELL AS IN THE DAY.
I'LL KEEP IN TOUCH WITH YOU.

WHAT'S GOING ON WITH MIZOGUCHI?

HIS GRANDSON WAS SAFELY RETURNED HOME.
MIZOGUCHI HIMSELF ISN'T FEELING WELL, SO HE'S TAKING TIME OFF FROM WORK.

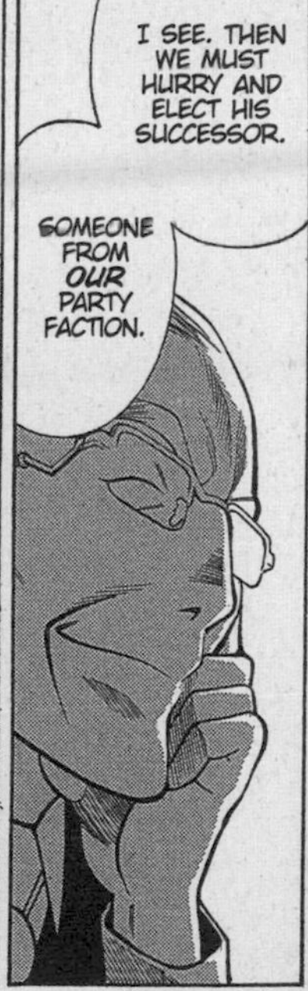
I SEE. THEN WE MUST HURRY AND ELECT HIS SUCCESSOR.
SOMEONE FROM *OUR* PARTY FACTION.

IT WAS A ROUGH WAY OF DOING IT, BUT WE'VE SUCCEEDED IN SHUTTING OUT THE OPPOSITION.
ALL FOR OUR HIGHNESS, THE PRINCESS.

AFTER THIS, WE CAN EXPECT THE ANTI-VAMPIRE PROPONENTS LURKING WITHIN THE OPPOSING FACTION TO DOUBLE THEIR EFFORTS IN STOPPING THE PRINCESS.

AND YOU THINK THAT'LL DESTROY HER? SHE'S TOUGH, YOU KNOW.
IT WON'T EVEN FAZE HER.

ACTUALLY, I'M MORE CONCERNED WITH THE ORGANIZATION THAT'S AFTER HER HIGHNESS.

"TELOMERE"... ISN'T THAT WHAT IT'S CALLED?
DO YOU THINK IT CONSISTS OF MEMBERS OF THE OPPOSITION?

I DON'T HAVE ANY DEFINITE PROOF, BUT FROM THE SHEER SCOPE AND SOPHISTICATION OF THE TWO PREVIOUS ASSASSINATION ATTEMPTS, IT'S CLEAR THAT IT'S A LARGE AND INFLUENTIAL ORGANIZATION.
IF THEY DECIDE TO MOVE OVERTLY AGAINST THE SPECIAL DISTRICT, THE IMPACT ON OUR COUNTRY WILL NOT BE SMALL.
HMM... IS THAT THE ONLY REASON YOU THINK THEY'RE IMPORTANT?
TAP
TAP
WHAT DO YOU MEAN BY THAT?

PER-HAPS...
YOU'RE LETTING NICOLE'S DEATH AFFECT YOU.
NO. I'M A PROFES-SIONAL.
AT ALL TIMES.

WELL, AS I SAID EARLIER, THE FUTURE OF OUR COUNTRY IS DEPENDANT ON THE SPECIAL DISTRICT.
AND FOR THAT REASON ALONE, WE NEED TO KEEP CLOSE SURVEILLANCE ON THE SPECIAL DISTRICT, AND TO KEEP THEM UNDER CONTROL.
THAT'S YOUR JOB. IT'S A SERIOUS RESPONSIBILITY, JOSIE.
I UNDER-STAND, GRAND-FATHER.

LATELY...
I'VE BEEN SPENDING A LOT OF TIME WITH THE PRINCESS.

SORRY FOR THE WAIT.

THE STUDENT MEETING ROOM AND CHAPEL WERE BOTH DESTROYED DURING "THE INCIDENT," SO WE'RE WITHOUT A BASE RIGHT NOW.
KEEP OUT KEEP OUT KEEP OUT
KEEP OUT KEEP OUT KEEP OUT KEEP

WE'RE REBUILDING, BUT IT'S GOING TO TAKE TIME...
WHY DON'T YOU USE THE DIRECTOR'S OFFICE?
IT'S RIDICULOUSLY BIG, AND IT GETS BORING SITTING IN THERE ALL BY MYSELF.
AND A LOT OF WORK.
DON'T BE SHY NOW! COME ON IN!

PTSD = POST-TRAUMATIC STRESS DISORDER

I PROMISED ALL THE SUPPORT I CAN GIVE, BUT...
SHE HAS TWO DIFFERENT FACES.
A KIND FACE THAT CONSIDERS THE FEELINGS OF THE WEAK...

AND A CRUEL ONE THAT ACTS WITHOUT HESITATION AT THE SLIGHTEST PROVOCATION.
AND THEN THERE'S ANOTHER... THE ONE SHE HAD WHEN SHE FOUGHT AKIRA-KUN.

BUT WHICH ONE IS HER TRUE FACE...?
!
I SEE. MY FACE FASCINATES YOU.
AH!

DON'T WORRY. YOURS IS *PRETTY* CUTE TOO.

H- HEY...
DON'T YOU SAVE THAT SORT OF THING FOR AKIRA-KUN?

FSSSH
AFTER I FIRST SAW HIM AGAIN, HE'D BE FLUSTERED EVERY TIME I SAID SOMETHING.
BUT FOR SOME REASON, LATELY *NOTHING* SEEMS TO BOTHER HIM.
IF I TEASED HIM LIKE THAT...
HE'D SAY, "YEAH, YEAH. THAT'S CUTE."
AND THAT WOULD BE IT.
GIGGLE
THAT'S A GOOD IMPRESSION.

I'M ALWAYS WITH HIM...
AND YET I NEVER TIRE OF LOOKING AT HIM.

BUT DON'T TELL HIM THAT.

....

WELL, I GUESS I NEED TO WRITE UP THE STUDENT COUNCIL APPLICATIONS...

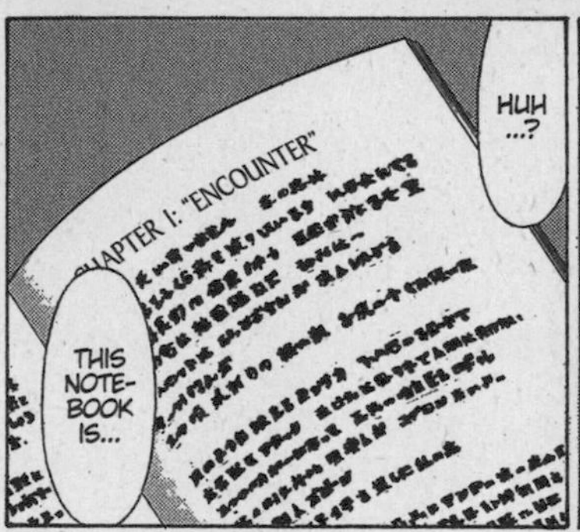
HUH ...?
CHAPTER 1: "ENCOUNTER"
THIS NOTEBOOK IS...

BAM

I...
I ACCIDENTALLY BROUGHT THE WRONG ONE!

AH...!
IT'S IN THE CLASS-ROOM...
I'LL... I'LL GO GET IT NOW!

BE RIGHT BACK!

....

OH... THAT WAS EMBAR-RASS-ING...
I CAN'T BELIEVE I BROUGHT *THAT* TO SCHOOL...
....
IT MAKES ME THINK, THOUGH...
WHY **DOES** THE PRINCESS KEEP ME AROUND ANYWAY?

AHHH!
OH. HEY.
A-AKIRA-KUN...!
GOOD TO SEE YOU.

UH, Y-YOU LEFT IN A HURRY AFTER SCHOOL THE OTHER DAY.
YEAH.

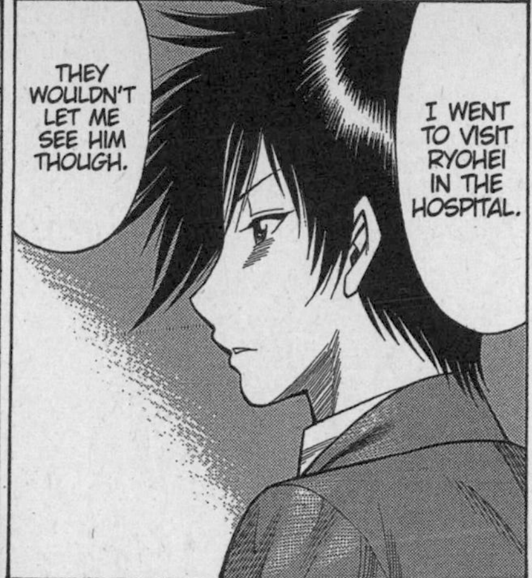
I WENT TO VISIT RYOHEI IN THE HOSPITAL.
THEY WOULDN'T LET ME SEE HIM THOUGH.

OH, I SEE...

......

EVER SINCE THAT NIGHT...
IT'S LIKE AKIRA-KUN HAS BEEN TRYING TO AVOID ME.

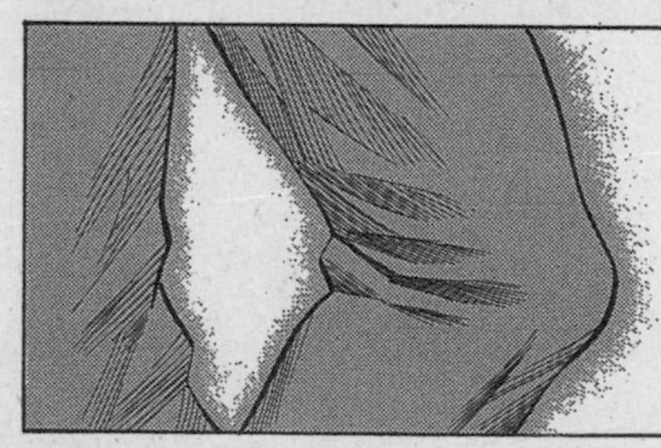

HOW LONG HAS IT BEEN...

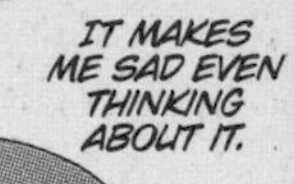
SINCE WE BOTH EVEN LAUGHED TOGETHER?

IT MAKES ME SAD EVEN THINKING ABOUT IT.
I FINALLY TOLD HIM MY FEELINGS, BUT...

I'M SORRY...

HE'S A WEREWOLF FROM "THE EARTH CLAN"...
AND ALSO THE PRINCESS'S OWN PERSONAL GUARDIAN.
I JUST HAD NO IDEA THAT AKIRA-KUN HAD ALL THESE RESPONSIBILITIES.

WE'LL BE TOGETHER... FOREVER.
THE PRINCESS WAS ALWAYS IN AKIRA-KUN'S HEART.
THERE WAS NEVER...
ANY ROOM FOR ME.
BUT...
IS THAT THE ONLY REASON?

PERHAPS THE REASON...
BUT DON'T TELL HIM THAT.
YUKI, WHAT'S WRONG?
TWITCH
SHE KEEPS ME AROUND IS TO SHOW ME THAT.
N-NOTHING...
I'M GOING TO GET MY BAG FROM THE CLASS-ROOM.
GO ON WITHOUT ME. I'LL MEET YOU THERE.
MAYBE I SHOULDN'T BE NEAR THE PRINCESS ANYMORE.
I MIGHT AS WELL QUIT THE STUDENT COUNCIL TOO.

SEEING THE TWO OF THEM TOGETHER...
IT'S JUST TOO PAINFUL.

HIME-SAMA...
I...

HIME-SAMA, THAT'S--!!
AHH!
SORRY, I WAS JUST...

SNATCH
D-DID YOU READ IT?
MM-HMM.
NOD NOD
I'M QUITE SURPRISED, TOO...
I DIDN'T KNOW YOU WROTE NOVELS.
BLUSH
かあっ

Y-YOU DIDN'T UNDERSTAND IT, RIGHT?
THERE'S ...A LOT OF *KANJI!*
I'VE BEEN STUDYING, SO I'VE GOTTEN TO THE POINT WHERE I CAN READ THE *MOST COMMONLY* USED KANJI.
AHHHHHHHH!

OH GOD...
THIS IS SO EMBARRASSING!

I'M REALLY SORRY...
I KNEW IT WAS RUDE OF ME TO READ WITHOUT PERMISSION.
BUT ONCE I STARTED READING IT, I COULDN'T STOP!
HUH?

YOU WRITE ENGAGING STORIES...
I GOT COMPLETELY CAUGHT UP IN IT.

LIAR...
WHY WOULD I LIE?
TRUST ME, I'VE READ EVERYTHING FROM *ULYSSES* TO *OLIVER TWIST*.

OF COURSE, I CAN'T SAY IT'S UP TO THE LEVEL OF BYRON OR RIMBAUD...
BUT YOUR WRITING IS FILLED WITH THE TENDERNESS AND SPARKLE OF A NOVICE.
THAT'S YOUR TRUE NATURE.
IT'S NOT SOME-THING YOU CAN LEARN TO DO.
NO...
YOU'RE JUST FLATTERING ME...
I CAN SENSE THESE THINGS.

YOU... SHED TEARS FOR ME.
NO, AKIRA-KUN, STOP!
SHE'S CRYING!
EVEN THOUGH I THREATENED YOU AND HELD YOU PRISONER.
YOU'RE A KIND GIRL WHO KNOWS COURAGE AND PRUDENCE.
IF I WERE TO HAVE A FRIEND, I'D *ALWAYS* WANT SOMEONE LIKE YOU.

AHH...
UHN...

H-
HUH?!
WHY ARE YOU CRYING?!

I...
I'M NOT THAT GOOD OF A PERSON.
BECAUSE I... DOUBTED YOU, HIME-SAMA.

YOU DON'T HAVE TO FEEL BADLY.
COME ON. LET'S PUT THE PIECES BACK TOGETHER.
YOU NEVER KNOW. SOMETHING GOOD MIGHT COME OF IT.

THEN, WE'RE...
"BOSOM FRIENDS"?
AS IN MONTGOMERY'S *ANNE OF GREEN GABLES*, HMM?
UNFORTUNATELY, I DON'T HAVE RED HAIR *OR* ANY FRECKLES. BUT IF THAT'S OKAY WITH YOU...

I'D LOVE TO!

BY THE WAY, I HAVE SOMETHING TO ASK YOU.
WHAT'S THAT?
I DIDN'T QUITE UNDERSTAND THE MARGIN NOTES IN YOUR STORY.
LIKE "SASOI-UKE," AND "KYOU-SEME," AND "CP"...
AND "SATOU"...
WHAT DOES THAT MEAN? IS IT SOME KIND OF CODE?
きゃあああ
AAAAHHH!!!...

WH-WHAT DID YOU SAY?!
HEY! WHAT ARE YOU DOING?
NOOOO!!
HEY.
READY TO GO, HIME-SAN?

UH...
WHAT'S GOING ON HERE?

OH... N-NOTHING!
RIGHT, HIME-SAMA?
WHISPER
PLEASE DON'T TELL AKIRA-KUN ABOUT MY STORY, OKAY?
ALL RIGHT... I KNOW!

YOU KNOW, YUKI...
IF HIME-SAN BULLIES YOU, YOU CAN JUST LET ME KNOW.

BULLYING IS ENTIRELY DISRE-SPECT-ABLE.
ESPECIALLY TOWARDS CUTE GIRLS.
YEAH, YEAH.
THAT'S CUTE.

HEE HEE HEE!
GIGGLE
?

YOU GUYS ARE CREEPING ME OUT.
I THOUGHT YOU DIDN'T LIKE EACH OTHER?

THAT'S NOT TRUE.
RIGHT, HIME-SAMA?

EXACTLY.
WE'RE BOSOM FRIENDS!

SINCE WHEN...?

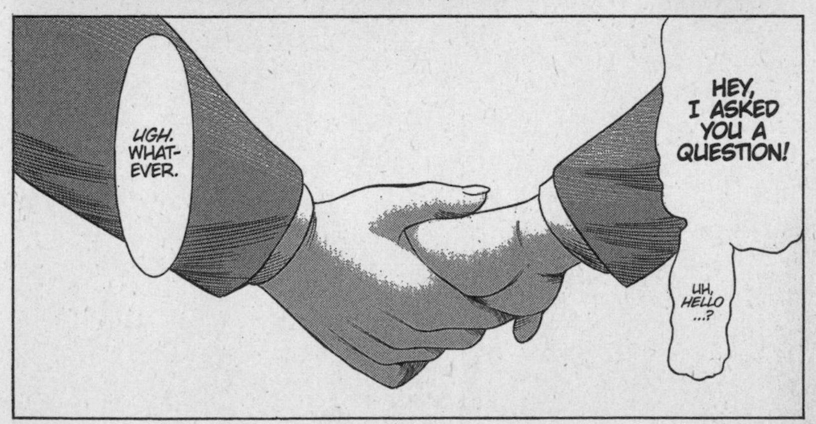
HEY, I ASKED YOU A QUESTION!
UH, HELLO ...?
UGH. WHAT-EVER.

SHUT UP! I DON'T CARE ABOUT YOUR SITUATION!
YOU'RE THE ONE THAT USED UP ALL THE MONEY!
GO DOWN TO THE FUZOKU THEN! GO SELL YOURSELF THERE!!
DO WHATEVER YOU HAVE TO DO TO GET THE MONEY, AND BRING IT TO ME!
SHIT! THAT BITCH!!
IF I LOSE MY PLACE AT THE TOP, I'LL KILL HER!!
!

HOOOONK
BEEEEEEP
VROOOOM
HAAAH
HAAAH
HAAAH
RUSTLE
HAAAH

CLANK
CLATTER
HEH HEH ...
YOU'RE PRETTY BOLD, HUH?
EVEN THOUGH YOU LOOK LIKE THE QUIET TYPE...
THIS ISN'T YOUR FIRST TIME, IS IT?!
AHHHH!
MHM!
SPREAD YOUR LEGS!!
MNH.
MNHH.
UHNN.
AHH...

ぎゃあああ
GYAAAAAAAAAH!
AH!
WHA ...
STOP!
AGHH!
SPLIIIK
SPLUURT

SPLOOSH
NAHH... AHH!
AGH.
SHVR
SHVR
DRIP DRIP
AHHHHHHHHHHH!!!
HAAH
HAAH
HAAH
UHN... I...
AAH...
MHN ...
TMP

YOU FINALLY DID IT, MY LITTLE PIGGY.
COME...
STAGGER
I...
HIC.
YES.

Chapter 14: Moving Shadows

ゴォォ..
RUMBLE

BEWARE OF VAMPIRES IN THE CITY!!
IS THE PERSON NEXT TO YOU REALLY HUMAN?
THE VAMPIRE ARMY IS HERE
TOKYO IS THEIR HUNTING GROUND!
HEEEEEY!
HEY, YOU!
CHECK THAT OUT!

SHE'S ALL DRESSED UP AND NOWHERE TO GO!
HEY, CUTIE.

WHATCHA DOIN' OUT THIS LATE?
YEAH, YOU SHOULDN'T BE RIDIN' ALL ALONE LIKE THAT.

YEP, I HEARD THERE'S BEEN *VAMPIRES* ON THESE SUBWAYS LATELY.
BUNCH OF PASSENGERS HAVE GONE MISSIN', TOO.
EVERYONE'S SCARED, SO THAT'S WHY IT'S SO *EMPTY* TONIGHT.
Z Z Z...

AREN'T YOU AFRAID? I WOULDN'T COME HERE ALONE.
......
ARE YOU GUYS VAMPIRES?
HEH!
YEAH RIGHT!

NAAAH, WE'RE JUST HUMANS!
I'LL *BITE* YA IF YA WANT ME TO, THOUGH!
OH, WAS I WRONG?
GOOD TO HEAR IT!
FWSSHH

HUH?
TMP
TMP
ER...
WHA...?
TMP
CRACK
GAAH!

ATTENTION PASSENGERS, ALL TRAIN SERVICE AT THIS STATION HAS BEEN TEMPORARILY SUSPENDED.
WE APOLOGIZE FOR ANY INCONVENIENCE AND WISH TO THANK YOU FOR YOUR PATIENCE.
WELL, THAT WAS A WASTE.

IT'S SO HARD TO FIND THE REAL THING OUT HERE.

DO YOU THINK IT'S TRUE THAT VAMPIRES ARE PROWLING AROUND, OUTSIDE OF THE BUND?

I DON'T KNOW.
BUT THERE HAVE BEEN A LOT OF UNEXPLAINED DISAPPEARANCES LATELY IN THE CITY.

BUT IS IT *REALLY* NECESSARY FOR YOU TO COME YOURSELF?
SOMETHING'S BEEN BOTHERING ME...
I HAVE A REASON FOR INVESTIGATING THIS MYSELF.

A REASON ...?
WAIT. HERE COMES A *NOISY* COMPLICATION.
YOUR HIGHNESS, I NEED TO SPEAK WITH YOU.
THIS CANNOT WAIT!!
SHE LOOKS REALLY PISSED OFF.
HM, YOU'RE RIGHT.

お手洗
Toilets

お手洗
BZZZ
FLICKR

YOU!

WHAT ARE YOU DOING HERE?
SHOULDN'T YOU BE IN SCHOOL?
GUIDANCE OFFICER
U-UMM...

I'M LOOKING ...
FOR SOMEONE ...
DID THEY GET LOST?
IT'S DANGEROUS TO BE ALONE. THERE MIGHT BE VAMPIRES.
TH-THE PERSON I'M LOOKING FOR...

IS A VAMPIRE!!

SO I THOUGHT IF I LOOKED AROUND HERE, I'D FIND HER...
HMM ...

IT'S MY LUCKY DAY.
YOU MIGHT COME IN HANDY!!
ACK!!
GRAB
AHHHHHH!!

TWITCH
SHLIK
HOW DARE YOU EXPOSE YOUR FANGS IN FRONT OF SOMEONE!
ARE YOU ALL RIGHT?
UGH ...
AGH ...
HE DIDN'T BITE YOU, DID HE?

YES.
YES.
駅長室
STATION MAS
WELL DONE.
THAT WAS VERA. SHE CAPTURED ONE.
LOOKS LIKE OUR EFFORTS WEREN'T FUTILE AFTER ALL.
EVEN SO, YOU CANNOT JUST ACT ON YOUR OWN LIKE THIS!
THE GOVERNMENT IS ALREADY PLANNING A COUNTER-MEASURE AFTER THIS INCIDENT...

YES, AND WHILE THE GOVERNMENT IS DRAGGING ITS FEET, THE VAMPIRES WILL CONTINUE TO MULTIPLY!
IF YOU WANT IT DONE RIGHT, YOU NEED TO LEAVE IT TO US.

THERE'S A POSSIBILITY THAT THE VAMPIRES HIDDEN IN THE CITY WERE ONES WHO ESCAPED FROM THE SPECIAL DISTRICT!
THAT'S EVEN MORE REASON FOR US TO CONFIRM IT!!
THE BUND HAS AN ABSOLUTE BORDER.
IT'S FORBIDDEN TO CROSS IT AND LEAVE!!

NOW, NOW.
YOU BOTH NEED TO CALM DOWN.

IT'S NOT LIKE WE'RE *ENEMIES* OR ANYTHING.

AND YOU ARE?

INSPECTOR HAMASEIJI.
THE CENTRAL GOVERNMENT OFFICE DISPATCHED HIM TO WORK *EXCLUSIVELY* ON THIS CASE.
YO!

YOU'RE THE ONLY ONE ON THIS CASE?
DON'T YOU THINK THAT'S A LITTLE... *OPTIMISTIC?*
YUP, YOU NAILED IT.
THINK OF ME AS YOUR *LIAISON* BETWEEN YOU AND THEM.
GOTCHA.

YOU KNOW HOW THE CENTRAL OFFICE IS. THEY'D MUCH RATHER JUST PASS THE BUCK ONTO SOMEONE ELSE.
NOBODY WANTS TO INVESTIGATE A BUNCH OF **VAMPIRES.** NOBODY'S *THAT* STUPID, WHICH IS WHY I'M HERE.

WELL, MR. FOOT-IN-YOUR-MOUTH, WHAT ARE YOU PLANNING ON DOING *NOW?*
OR HAD YOU NOT THOUGHT THAT FAR AHEAD?
OH CRAP!
WELL, I *DO* HAVE THE VAMPIRE THAT THE REALLY HOT LADY CAUGHT. SHOVED HIM IN AN EMPTY ROOM WITHOUT ANYTHING TO DRINK.
BET HE'S PRETTY THIRSTY BY NOW. MIGHT BE READY TO TALK. *SO,* WHO WANTS TO GO AND ASK HIM A FEW QUESTIONS?
I'LL SEE HIM.

CREAK

AKIRA.
POINT POINT

GNNG...
AGH...
GRAB
GAUUUHH!
FSSHH!

HUFF
HUFF
NOW... WHEN YOU'VE CALMED DOWN, YOU NEED TO ANSWER ME.

DID YOU ESCAPE FROM THE BUND?

....

9
WHY WON'T YOU ANSWER ...?
WELL, THIS IS A NEW ONE.
HE WON'T ANSWER MY QUESTION.

CURRENTLY, ALL THE VAMPIRES IN THIS COUNTRY SHOULD BE BOUND BY THEIR OATH TO MY FAMILY.
THERE SHOULDN'T BE ANYONE WHO CAN DISOBEY MY ORDERS.

WHERE...
ARE YOU FROM?
WHO IS YOUR MASTER?
IS IT LI?
IVA-NOVIC?
OR COULD IT BE...

GRAAAAH!
BLERRH!
GAK!
CLANG
!
HIME-
SAN!!
GLOTCH
BWOOOM!!

HIME-
SAMA!!

I'M FINE...
AKIRA PROTECTED ME.

BUT IT WOULD SEEM OUR VAMPIRE FRIEND BLEW HIMSELF UP.
BUT THAT'S IMPOS-SIBLE...!
WE SEARCHED HIS BODY INSIDE AND OUT FOR EXPLOSIVES! METAL DETECTORS, CAVITY SEARCHES AND ALL!

WELL, *APPARENTLY* THEY'VE FOUND A WAY TO STUFF PLASTIC EXPLOSIVES INSIDE OF THEIR *STOMACHS.* SO I'D SUGGEST **X-RAYING** HIM NEXT TIME.
ANYWAY, VERA...

WE'VE GOT TROUBLE ON OUR HANDS.
IT LOOKS LIKE THE THIRD CLAN IS INVOLVED.
!

UM...
I HATE TO INTERRUPT... BUT COULD ONE OF YOU BRING ME SOME CLOTHES?

FWOMP
PHEW!!

THANKS, YUKI.
THESE CLOTHES FIT PERFECTLY.
AH, GOOD!

BUT HOW'D YOU GUESS MY SIZE?
WELL ...
THE PRINCESS TOLD ME.
SHE DIDN'T TELL YOU ANYTHING... *WEIRD,* DID SHE?
OF COURSE NOT!
HIME-SAN...?

I SEE...
YOU WERE LOOKING FOR A FRIEND OF YOURS THAT WAS TURNED INTO A VAMPIRE.
THAT'S A BIT RECK-LESS.
IF VERA HADN'T SAVED YOU, YOU'D BE ONE OF US NOW.
......

I JUST WANTED...
TO SEE ONEECHAN AGAIN.

ONEE-CHAN?
YOU MEAN YOUR SISTER?
NO, BUT SHE'S LIKE A SISTER TO ME.
WE'RE NEIGHBORS, AND WE'VE BEEN CLOSE EVER SINCE I WAS LITTLE.
CHILD-HOOD FRIENDS?

LITTLE BOY, THERE'S NO GUARANTEE THAT SHE'S THE SAME GIRL YOU REMEMBER.
WHEN YOU BECOME A VAMPIRE, YOU CHANGE. SHE MIGHT'VE ALREADY FORGOTTEN ABOUT...

THAT'S NOT TRUE! ONEECHAN HASN'T FORGOTTEN ME!!

ONEECHAN... SHE... SHE CAME TO SEE ME.
SHE DIDN'T STAY LONG, THOUGH...
!

WHEN WAS THIS?!
UM, THE DAY BEFORE YESTER-DAY...

HIME-SAMA!
SO, THE THREAD WE THOUGHT BROKEN WAS STILL CONNECTED IN AN UNEXPECTED WAY. HMM...

AS IT STANDS, THERE ARE VAMPIRES ON THE MAINLAND.
THEY'RE OBVIOUSLY CONNECTED TO OUR ENEMY SOMEHOW.

YOU SAID YOUR NAME IS YUZURU-KUN, RIGHT?
CAN YOU TELL US MORE ABOUT THIS GIRL? STARTING WITH HER NAME.
HER NAME...
IS SHINO-NOME...
SHINONOME NANAMI.
SHINONOME NANAMI...
THAT SOUNDS FAMILIAR ...
YUKI?

THAT'S KAICHOU'S ...
THE STUDENT COUNCIL PRESIDENT'S NAME!
!

KAICHOU IS...
OUR ENEMY?!

THREE DAYS EARLIER ——
AH!
MOM! ARE THE NEIGHBORS MOVING?!
THE SHINO-NOMES? IT SEEMS THAT WAY.
I GUESS THEY HAVE NO CHOICE. ONE OF THEM TURNED INTO A VAMPIRE...
IT MUST BE HARD FOR THEM. EVERYONE'S TALKING ABOUT IT.
Tp Tp Tp
NO WAY...
WELL ...

TO TELL YOU THE TRUTH, I'M RELIEVED.
WHO KNOWS WHETHER OR NOT THAT GIRL INFECTED ANYONE ELSE IN HER FAMILY?
Tp Tp Tp
THE GOVERN-MENT IS LOOKING INTO IT, I HEAR.
EVEN IF THAT'S NOT THE CASE, IT'S STILL CREEPY.
THIS IS BEST FOR EVERY-ONE.
NO...
WHAT'S GONNA HAPPEN WHEN NANAMI-ONEECHAN COMES BACK?!
WHAT ARE YOU TALKING ABOUT?
ONCE A HUMAN BECOMES A VAMPIRE, THEY'RE SENT TO THE SPECIAL DISTRICT. THEY AREN'T ALLOWED TO RETURN.
YOU NEED TO FORGET ABOUT HER ALREADY.
SHE WAS ALWAYS GOOD TO YOU, BUT SHE'S NOT *HUMAN* ANYMORE.

ONEE...
CHAN
...
YUZURU-
CHAN...
YUZURU...
HN?
CREAK
...

O-ONEE-CHAN...?

NNM!
MMPH...
MM.
NH.
MMPH...
AH...
ONEE...
HUFF
HUFF

AHHH!
OH NO...
AH...
CLASP
ONEECHAN!

Chapter 15: Children of the Night

ONEECHAN...

NANAMI-ONEECHAAAAAAAAN!!!

THERE DOES SEEM TO BE RECORD OF SHINONOME NANAMI ENTERING THE SPECIAL DISTRICT.

BUT THE BOY SAID HE SAW HER THREE DAYS AGO...
I KNOW.

WOLFGANG-DONO CHECKED OUT THE PLACE WHERE SHE WAS ASSIGNED TO LIVE...
THERE WAS NO TRACE OF ANYONE HAVING LIVED THERE. IT'S LIKELY THAT SHE HAS NEVER EVEN BEEN THERE.
Tp Tp
PERHAPS SHE WENT MISSING AFTER ENTERING THE SPECIAL DISTRICT.
WHAT ABOUT THE OTHER STUDENTS?

SAME THING.
ACCORDING TO IMMIGRATION RECORDS, AROUND TEN OF THEM HAVE ALSO GONE MISSING.
SO THESE STUDENTS ARE THE CULPRITS BEHIND THE SUBWAY ATTACKS?
THEY DON'T LOOK LIKE THE TYPE TO ME.

MAYBE SOMEONE HELPED THEM TO ESCAPE BEFORE THEY ENTERED THE ISLAND, AND THEN RECRUITED THEM.

THINK ABOUT IT. DO YOU THINK THEY COULD FALSIFY THESE RECORDS THEMSELVES?
IT WOULD HAVE TO BE A VERY POWERFUL ORGANIZATION THAT COULD TAKE THAT NUMBER OF VAMPIRES AWAY WITHOUT US NOTICING.
AN ORGA-NIZA-TION...?
WHAT WAS THAT NAME AGAIN...
COULD IT BE TELOMERE?
NO, NOT THIS TIME.
WHY'S THAT?

AT THIS POINT, I THINK THEIR OBJECTIVE IS *MY LIFE.*
THAT'S DIFFERENT FROM TELOMERE, WHOSE PLAN WAS TO CORRUPT HUMAN SOCIETY.
OH...
THEN WHO ELSE COULD IT BE?

I CAN THINK OF MANY PEOPLE WHO WOULD WANT ME DEAD.
BOTH HUMANS...
HMPH
AND VAMPIRES.
DIDN'T YOU SAY BEFORE...
THAT THE **THIRD CLAN** WAS INVOLVED?
THE... *OTHER* ROYAL FAMILY?
AKIRA.

I CAN'T BE ENTIRELY SURE YET.
WE NEED TO INVESTIGATE FURTHER TO SEE IF WE CAN FIND ANY DEFINITE PROOF.

BUT WE SHOULD MAKE A MOVE BEFORE THEY DO. KEEP THEM OFF-BALANCE.
HAVING MORE PEOPLE SENT FROM THE BUND WOULD JUST BE ADDING OIL TO THE FIRE.
NO. I'LL WORK WITH THE PEOPLE WE ALREADY HAVE OUT.
ALSO ...

I'LL TAKE RESPONSIBILITY FOR NANAMI.
WE CAN'T LEAVE HER ALONE.

......

?
WHAT'S WRONG, YUKI?

I CAN'T BELIEVE THAT KAICHOU HAS ANYTHING TO DO WITH THESE ATTACKS...
AFTER JEAN MARAIS DIED, SHE WAS SET FREE OF HIS MIND CONTROL.
I THOUGHT SHE'D CHOOSE A PEACEFUL LIFE BY LIVING AS A FANGLESS VAMPIRE.

BECAUSE IT JUST DOESN'T SEEM LIKE...
KAICHOU COULD *DO* THIS.

PERHAPS SHE'S BEING **FORCED** TO COMMIT THESE ACTS BECAUSE SHE'S UNDER ANOTHER MASTER'S CONTROL.
BUT SHE DOES HAVE FEELINGS, TOO.
SHE MAY BE *SUFFERING* FROM UNCON-TROLLABLE DESIRES THAT WE CAN'T EVEN IMAGINE.
DE-SIRES ...?
LIKE... WHAT?

OH... I-I SEE...

HIME-SAMA! THEY'RE HERE!!
FSSH

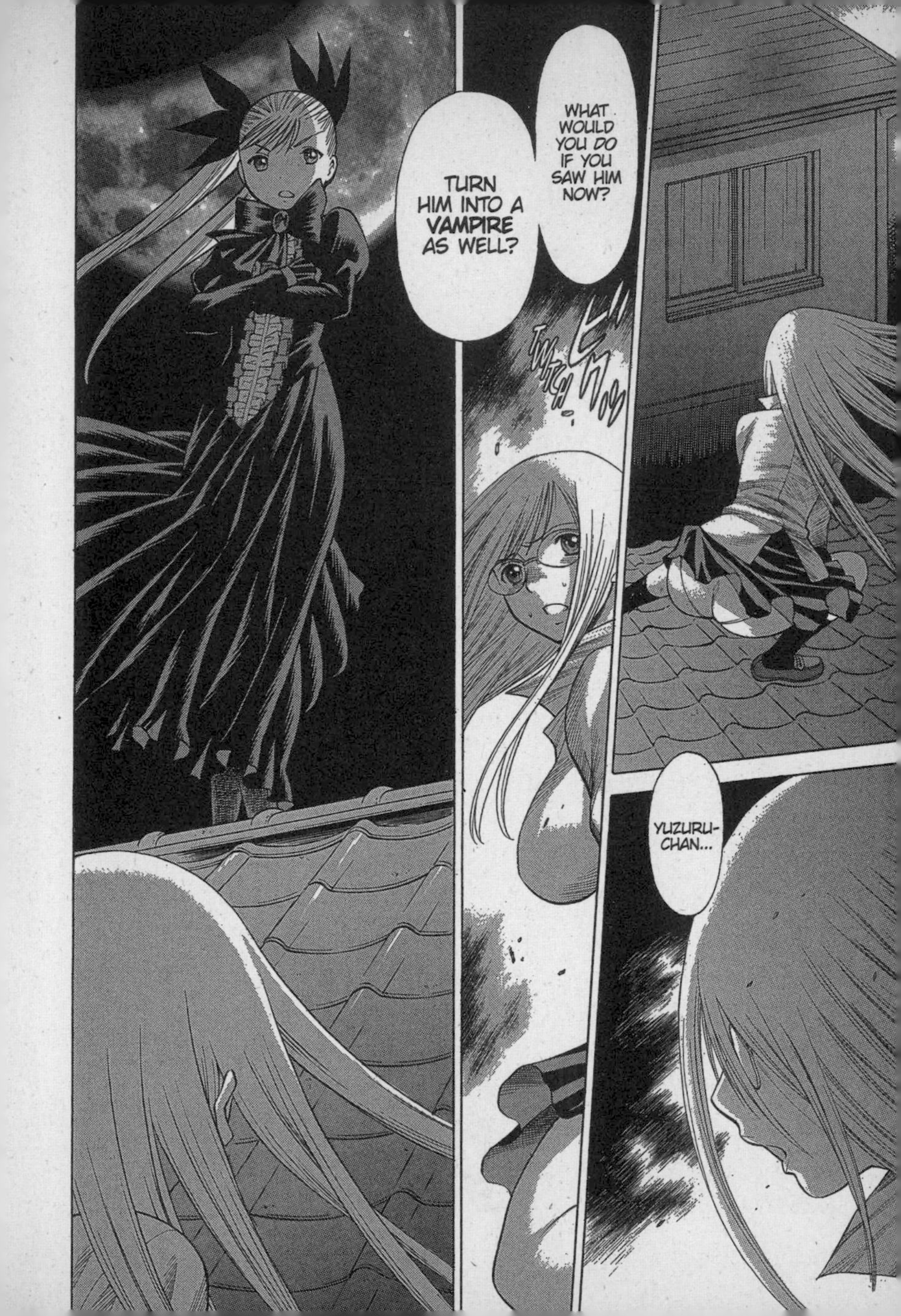
WHAT WOULD YOU DO IF YOU SAW HIM NOW?
TURN HIM INTO A VAMPIRE AS WELL?
TWITCH
YUZURU-CHAN...

Y- YOUR HIGHNESS ...
TO THINK YOU'VE DONE SUCH *TERRIBLE THINGS* AFTER I LET YOU OUT OF MY SIGHT.
TMP
!

IN ACCORDANCE WITH THE TEPES BLOOD PACT, YOU MUST OBEY THE ORDERS OF THE SOVEREIGN.
NANAMI SHINONOME, YOU WILL RETURN TO THE BUND WITH ME IMMEDIATELY.

WHAT ...?
YOU DARE TO DISOBEY ME?
UGH...
AGH...
HIISSSS!
I KNEW IT! YOU'VE BEEN OVERWRITTEN!!
AKIRA !!
SNF
TP
GLEAM
YOU CAN'T RUN, KAICHOU!

FWOOSH
CRACK
ARGH!!
AKIRA!
YOU INSOLENT CHILD!
TMP
HIME-SAN!!
I'M FINE!
VERA-SAN!!
THERE ARE TROOPS IN AMBUSH NEARBY! SEND BACKUP!!
!
WHERE'S HIME-SAMA?!

SHE FOL-LOWED HER!!
SHE WHAT?!
AKIRA, YOU MUST KEEP HER IN SIGHT AT ALL COSTS!!
WE CAN'T AFFORD TO LOSE HER HIGH-NESS!!
FWOOSH
GOD, WHAT A NUI-SANCE...
THAT HAMASEIJI SHOULD BE WATCHING HIS OWN DAMN SUR-VEILLANCE FEEDS!
TMP

ONEE-CHAN...
HUFF
HUFF

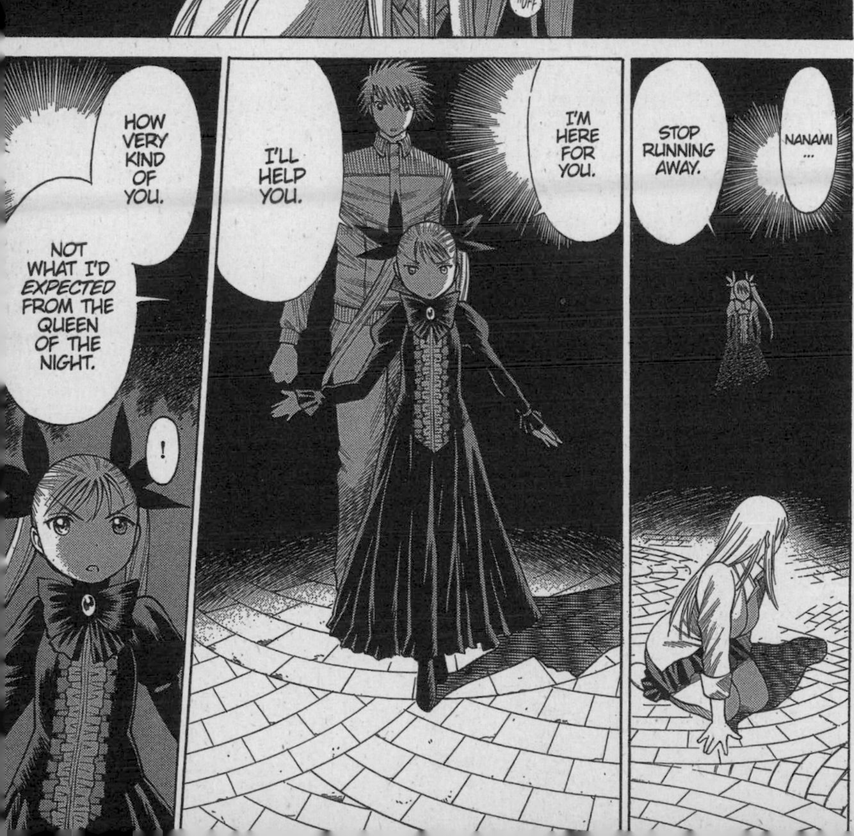
NANAMI...
STOP RUNNING AWAY.
I'M HERE FOR YOU.
I'LL HELP YOU.
HOW VERY KIND OF YOU.
NOT WHAT I'D *EXPECTED* FROM THE QUEEN OF THE NIGHT.
!

"IF YOU SEND THIS GIRL, HER HIGHNESS WILL MAKE AN APPEARANCE HERSELF."
HEH. HONESTLY, I HAD MY DOUBTS THAT IT WOULD EVEN WORK.
I MEAN, TO THINK THAT PRINCESS *MINA* WOULD FEEL LIKE SHE *OWES* SOMETHING TO THIS MERE FEMALE VAMPIRE...
IT'S PITIFUL.

ARE YOU HER NEW MASTER?
I DON'T RECOG-NIZE YOU.
IT'S OUR FIRST MEETING.
MY NAME IS HYSTERICA. IT'S A *PLEASURE* TO MEET YOU.

SAME HERE.
WELL? WHY HAVE YOU COME TO THIS COUNTRY, MISS HYSTERICA?
ARE YOU PLANNING ON *GATHERING* VAMPIRES...
TO INCREASE YOUR NUMBERS?

HEH! I'VE MADE A LOT OF PREPARA-TIONS FOR THIS MOMENT...
AND IT LOOKS LIKE THEY'RE ABOUT TO PAY OFF.
COME WITH ME NOW.
IF YOU SIMPLY *ACCEPT* MY MASTER, IT'LL ALL BE OVER.

MASTER ...?
IT LOOKS LIKE YOU KNOW ME WELL.
HEH.
GET BACK, HIME-SAN!
AH. YOU MUST BE THE WEREWOLF. YOU'RE SO LOYAL, SO BRAVE.
HOW-EVER...

THE ODDS ARE IN... MY FAVOR.

H-HOW DID SO MANY...?

!
HIKO ...?!

......
HEAR ME!
THERE ARE SOME HERE WHO WISHED TO BECOME VAMPIRES.

SURRENDER TO ME AND JOIN OUR KINGDOM.
IF YOU DO, I SWEAR TO PROTECT YOU WITH ALL THE POWER AT MY DISPOSAL.

ARE YOU BLIND?!
STOP ACTING SO NOBLE AND VIRTUOUS!!
EVEN IF YOU ARE THE QUEEN OF ALL VAMPIRES, I DON'T BELIEVE IT!
WHAT DO YOU MEAN "IF"? I MOST CERTAINLY AM THE QUEEN OF ALL VAMPIRES.
I'D WATCH MY TONGUE IF I WERE YOU, LITTLE GIRL.
IT BETRAYS YOUR TRUE CHARACTER...
AND IT'S GIVING ME AN IDEA OF JUST WHERE YOU'RE FROM.
!
ATTACK!!

!
FWOOSH
CRACK
SWIPE
SWISH

WHAT ??
FWMP
FWISH
FWOOM
THUMP

WE'RE THE ELITE EIGHT.
LORD REGENDORF INSTRUCTED US TO COME AND PROTECT YOUR HIGHNESS.

VERY WELL. YOU MAY CARRY OUT YOUR MISSION.
FINALLY ...
I GET TO SEE THE QUEEN'S LOYAL LAPDOGS.
DON'T HESIS-TATE!
RAAAH!
LET THE SKY RAIN WITH BLOOD !!

ORDERS, YOUR HIGHNESS?
DON'T TOUCH THE HEAD WOMAN OR THE GIRL.
THE FATE OF THE OTHERS IS INEVITABLE NOW.
TURN THEM INTO DUST!
AS YOU WISH !!
SHOW ME YOUR LOYALTY!!
LEAVE NO VAMPIRE STANDING!!

SWAAAHH
EN GARDE !!

HERE THEY COME, BROTHERS! YOUR HIGHNESS, PLEASE STAY BACK!
ABSO-LUTELY NOT!
WHAT KIND OF MASTER LEAVES HER KNIGHTS TO FIGHT ALONE?!
BESIDES, I STILL HAVE BUSINESS WITH THAT WOMAN OVER THERE.
AS YOU WISH !!

HER HIGHNESS HAS SPOKEN!
WE SHALL CUT A PATH FORWARD FOR YOU!!

Chapter 16: Werewolf ~Beowulf~

SWOOSH
AH HA HA HA HA!!
SLASH
SWIPE
SHIIK

SLASH
FWP
FWOOM

THMP
FWISH
THUD
GYAA!

JUST WHAT I'D EXPECT FROM WERE-WOLVES.
THEY'RE EXTRA-ORDINA--
FSSHH
!
MI...
BASH

SNATCH
MINA-HIMEEE!!!
!
SHOOMP
SHOOMP
FWOOSH
SWF

UNNH!
CRUNCH
NOW, HYSTERICA ...
I'M GOING TO NEED SOME ANSWERS !!

THMP
NA...
NANAMI!
AKIRA!
HIME-SAN! QUIT GOING OFF ON YOUR OWN!

!
NANAMI! THAT WAS HER!
COME BACK, NANAMI!
HIME-SA--
CRAAAK
YOU IGNORE ME FOR THAT LITTLE PIG?!
DON'T YOU DARE UNDER-ESTIMATE ME!
WHISSH

SMACK
VERA!!

GO AFTER HER, HIME-SAMA!!
LEAVE THIS TO ME!

YOU HEARD HER, AKIRA!
GOT IT!
AFTER HER!
TMP

WELL ...
DOESN'T THIS JUST BRING BACK MEMORIES?
VERATOS!!
THE LAST TIME I SAW YOU WAS IN 1900.
IT WAS 1918 IN PARIS, FRANCESCA.

CALL ME **HYSTERICA.** I LIKE THAT NAME BETTER NOW.

YOU CHANGED YOUR NAME *AGAIN?*
YOU'VE PROBABLY BEEN GOING FROM ONE MASTER TO THE NEXT, HUH?

I CAN'T BE SO WHOLE-HEARTEDLY *DEVOTED* TO ONE MASTER, LIKE YOU.
SO WHAT'S WITH THAT UGLY GET-UP?
I CAN HARDLY BELIEVE YOU'RE VERATOS, THE "BLACK RUBY" OF HIGH SOCIETY!

IF ONLY YOU HAD COME WITH ME BACK THEN...
YOU WOULD HAVE HAD *ANYTHING* YOU WANTED.
INSTEAD, YOU FELT AN OBLIGATION TO THAT LITTLE BRAT.
SHE'S A QUEEN IN *NAME ONLY.*
SO WHAT IF SHE'S BUILT A LITTLE *GARDEN* HERE IN THIS PUNY ISLAND COUNTRY?
SHE'S IN THE PALM OF MY MASTER'S HAND.

LITTLE CHILDREN SHOULD BE SEEN AND NOT HEARD BY THEIR ELDERS.
AND NOW I'M GOING TO **PUNISH** HER...
SILENCE!!

YOU SAID I COULD HAVE HAD ANYTHING?
FWOO

I DON'T NEED ANY-THING...
FLIK
BESIDES HIME-SAMA!!

HYSTERICA!
I'LL MAKE YOU *PAY* FOR THOSE WORDS!!

BRING IT ON!

FWISH
LET'S SETTLE THIS HERE AND NOW!!
NINETY YEARS WAS FAR TOO LONG!
!
SKSORY

AHH!
FWOOSH

!

THIS SCENT ...
A CHILD?
WHY ARE YOU HERE?

RUN AWAY. THIS IS NO PLACE FOR A CHILD.
UM...

HAVE YOU SEEN A GIRL WEARING GLASSES?
SHE'S IN HIGH SCHOOL, AND...

POINT
!

THANK YOU!

THAT WAS UN-EXPECTED.
......

"YOU CANNOT STOP THE FLOW OF WATER."
WHAT, ARE YOU A POET NOW?

ONEECHAN...
HUFF
HUFF
WHAT'S WRONG, YUZURU-KUN?

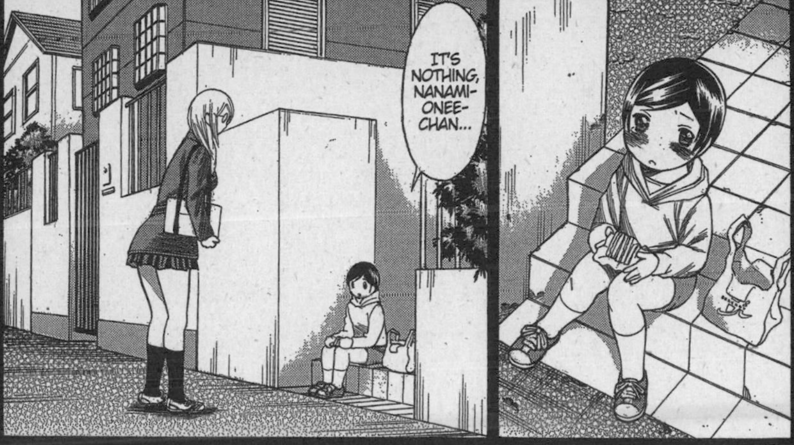
IT'S NOTHING, NANAMI-ONEE-CHAN...

JUST THAT MOM SAID IT WAS TOO MUCH TROUBLE TO COOK ME ANYTHING.
IS SHE DAY TRADING AGAIN...?
UGH, WHAT KIND OF MOTHER DOESN'T THINK ABOUT HER OWN SON?!
COME ON, ONEECHAN WILL MAKE YOU SOME DINNER.
WE CAN EAT TOGETHER.
IT'S OKAY?

OF COURSE.
NOBODY'S HOME AT MY PLACE EITHER.
AREN'T YOU LONELY, ONEECHAN?
NOPE.
BECAUSE I HAVE YOU, YUZURU-CHAN.
ONEECHAN...

DON'T GO...
DON'T GO, ONEECHAN!

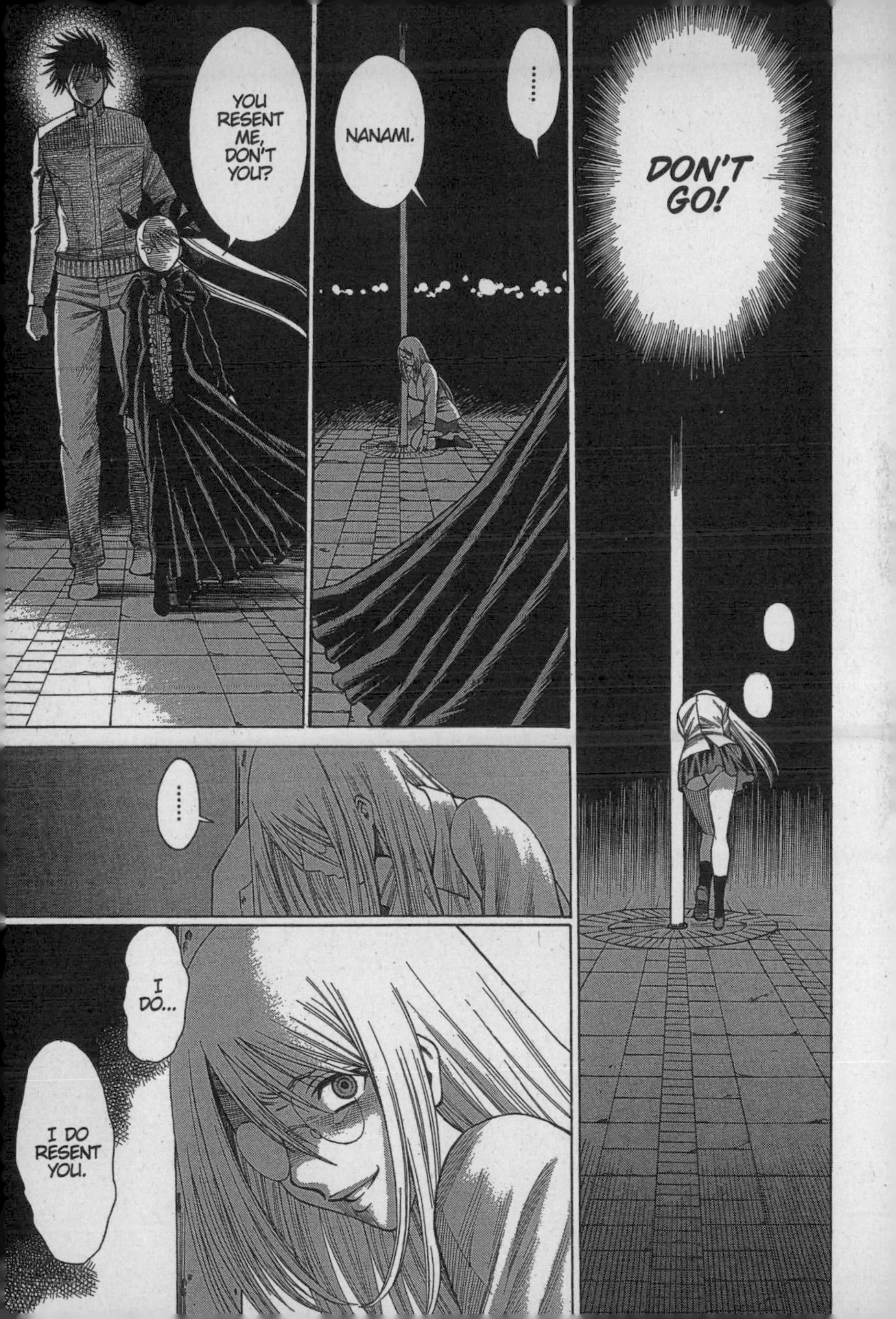
DON'T GO!
......
NANAMI.
YOU RESENT ME, DON'T YOU?
......
I DO...
I DO RESENT YOU.

NOT BECAUSE MY BODY'S LIKE THIS!!
I DON'T CARE ABOUT THAT!!
I ACTED LIKE I DIDN'T NOTICE!
I WAS TRYING TO HIDE IT SO MUCH!!

ARE YOU TALKING ABOUT THE BOY?
DON'T SAY IT!
IT'S TOO TERRI-BLE...
IF HE EVEN SUSPECTED I HAD SUCH SHAMEFUL FEELINGS, I...
BUT...

I CAN'T STOP IT! I CAN'T!
I FEEL MYSELF LONGING FOR HIM SO MUCH I WANT TO TEAR MY OWN CHEST OPEN!!
KILL ME...
DO IT NOW!
BEFORE I MAKE HIM DIRTY!
NANAMI ...
BEFORE HE STARTS TO HATE ME...
PLEASE ...KILL ME....
ONEE-CHAN...?

YUZURU-CHAN?
ONEE-CHAN!
NO!!

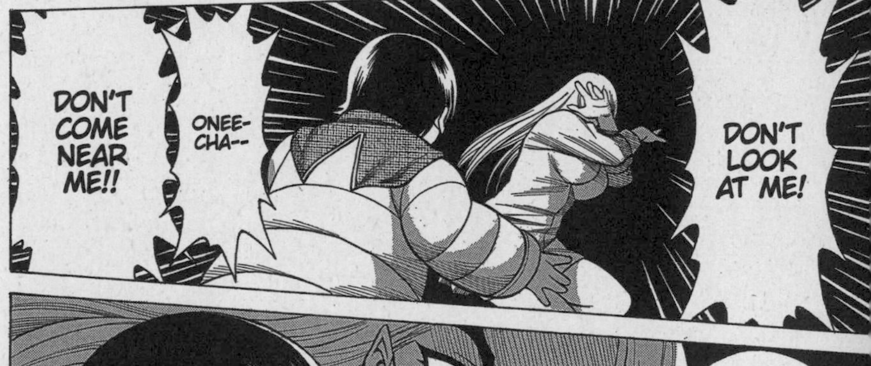
DON'T LOOK AT ME!
ONEE-CHA--
DON'T COME NEAR ME!!

DIDN'T YOU HEAR HER? SHE SAID TO GO AWAY!

SMACK
!
YUZURU-CHAN!
SNATCH
YUZURU-CHAN...
FWOOSH

VERA!!
I'M SORRY, HIME-SAMA.
I WAS TOO LATE.

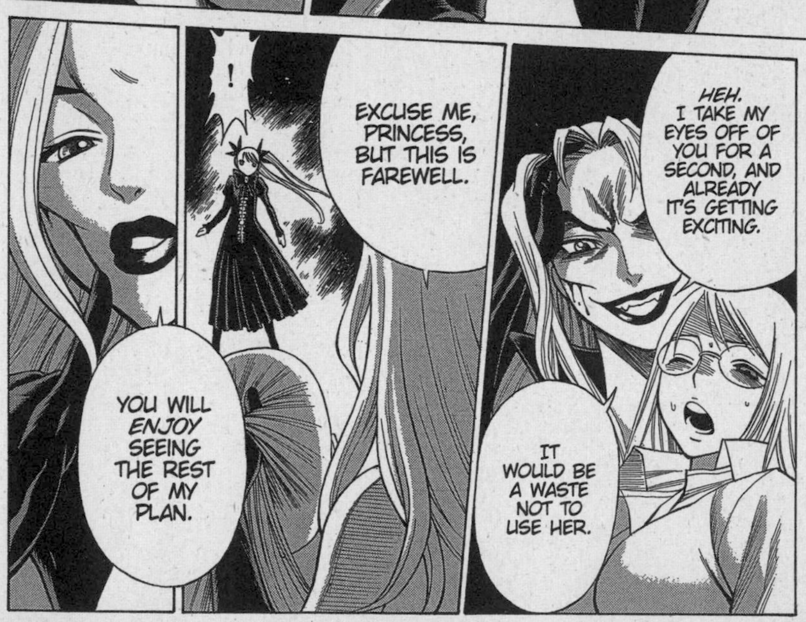
HEH. I TAKE MY EYES OFF OF YOU FOR A SECOND, AND ALREADY IT'S GETTING EXCITING.
IT WOULD BE A WASTE NOT TO USE HER.
!
EXCUSE ME, PRINCESS, BUT THIS IS FAREWELL.
YOU WILL ENJOY SEEING THE REST OF MY PLAN.

AKIRA, FOLLOW THEM!
I'M ON IT!!
TMP
TMP
OUT OF MY WAY!
PIP
GOOSH

SHOOOSH
KA-BLOOOSH
AKIRA!!
ANOTHER SUICIDE BOMBING ...?
RUMBLE
KOFF...
I-I'M FINE...

DAMN.
SHE GOT AWAY.

....

ONEE-CHAN...

....
HMM ...
YOUR HIGHNESS, ARE YOU SAFE?!

HOW DID IT GO?
THEY RETREATED.
BUT ONLY AFTER RECEIVING CONSIDERABLE DAMAGE.
MORE IMPORTANTLY, YOUR HIGHNESS ...

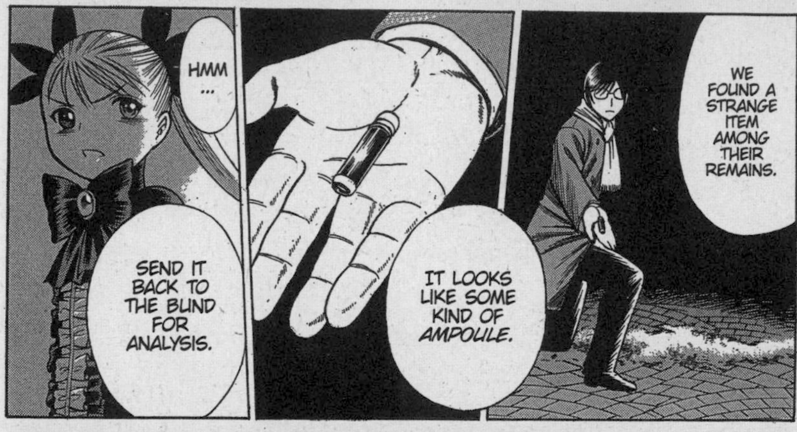
WE FOUND A STRANGE ITEM AMONG THEIR REMAINS.
IT LOOKS LIKE SOME KIND OF *AMPOULE*.
HMM ...
SEND IT BACK TO THE BUND FOR ANALYSIS.

BUT FIRST, WITHDRAW TO THE COMMAND POST.
IT'S BEST THAT WE ALLOW THINGS TO SETTLE HERE.

HIME-SAN...
IT'LL BE MORNING SOON. YOU SHOULD RETURN TO THE CAR.

AKIRA. YOU SAID BEFORE THAT YOU THOUGHT I DIDN'T GET ALONG WITH YUKI.
WHAT DID YOU MEAN?

UM ...
JUST A GUESS. IT'S NOTHING.
A GUESS ?
THEY SAY VAMPIRES WILL CORRUPT HUMAN SOCIETY IF THEY WERE LET LOOSE.
EVEN IF IT'S JUST A MYTH, IT DOESN'T REALLY DETER PEOPLE FROM VAMPIRES.

THE VAMPIRES ARE MULTIPLYING LIKE *RATS* IN THE BUND...
SURE, IT WOULD TAKE A LONG TIME FOR THEM TO TRULY **DAMAGE** HUMAN SOCIETY.
BUT DO YOU REALLY THINK THE AUTHORITIES CAN HANDLE IT? I DON'T THINK SO. THE RISK IS JUST TOO GREAT.

HEE HEE HEE.
WHAT?

I WAS JUST THINKING HOW *THOROUGHLY* WOLFGANG HAS TRAINED YOU.

IT HAS **NOTHING** TO DO WITH MY DAD!!
DON'T GET MAD.
I'M SAYING YOU'RE RIGHT.

THINK ABOUT TODAY'S BATTLE.
THEY HAD GONE TO ALL THAT TROUBLE TO INCREASE THEIR NUMBERS...
SO THAT THEY MIGHT CAPTURE ME FOR THEIR MASTER.
THAT **ALONE** CONVINCES ME.

WHATEVER THEIR PLAN IS, ADULT VAMPIRES AREN'T NECESSARY.
THAT... AND IT JUST *MIGHT* BE CARRIED OUT WITHIN THE NEXT DAY OR SO.

HOW CAN YOU BE SURE?
SHE SHOWED US HER CARDS. SHE'D ONLY DO THAT IF SHE WAS CLOSE TO SETTLING THIS.

IT WAS IN HER VOICE, TOO. SUCH SENSELESS HATRED.
SIGH... VAMPIRES ARE SO HOPELESS BY NATURE...

SO THE KID...

WHAT ARE YOU GOING TO DO ABOUT HIM, HIME-SAN?

YOU MEAN YUZURU?

YEAH, HE SHOULD BE SENT HOME TO HIS PARENTS.
HE SHOULDN'T GET INVOLVED ANY FURTHER.

HE COULD LEAVE NOW WITHOUT ANY CONSE- QUENCES...
BUT WHAT ABOUT TOMORROW ?
....

I HEARD FROM COUNCILOR GOTOH... SOME TV STATION TOOK A SURVEY.
"WOULD YOU LIKE TO BECOME A VAMPIRE?"

OVER 30% OF PEOPLE ANSWERED YES.
AND THE MOST POPULAR REASON WAS... "SO I CAN LIVE FOREVER."

ACTUALLY...
MANY PEOPLE THINK THAT THE LATEST SACRIFICES WERE PEOPLE WHO WENT *LOOKING* TO GET ATTACKED.

HOW FOOLISH... ETERNITY IS LIKE THE NEVER-ENDING FLOW OF A GREAT RIVER.
IF YOU DON'T HAVE SOMETHING TO HOLD ONTO, IT'LL PULL YOU UNDER WITH ALL ITS SORROWS.

SO HAVING THAT ONE THING TO HOLD ONTO...
MAKES ALL THE DIFFER-ENCE.

HIME-SAN...

YES.
YES.
I SEE... THAT'S WHAT I SUS-PECTED.
NEWS?
YES, CALL UP BEOWULF.
THE ANALYSIS OF THAT AMPOULE IS COMPLETE.

I KNOW WHAT THEY'RE PLOTTING!!
NOW IT'S TIME FOR OUR COUNTER-STRIKE!!

YOU LOOK GOOD LIKE THAT, *LITTLE PIGGY.*
IT SUITS YOUR BLISTER-ING SOUL!
AHH ...

I'LL MAKE YOUR DREAMS COME TRUE.

Chapter 17: Strategic Chess Game

REGARDING THE RECENT VAMPIRE ATTACKS, I OFFER MY HEARTFELT APOLOGIES TO ALL OF THE CITIZENS OF TOKYO.

ヴァンパイア襲撃事件
都民の皆様に心より陳謝いたします。

BUT THAT'S...

A CHALLENGE TO HYSTERICA.

OUR HIME-SAN HAS SOME GUTS, I'LL GIVE HER THAT.

TEN HOURS EARLIER——

YOU MAY RECALL THAT AN AMPOULE WAS FOUND AMONGST THE REMAINS OF ONE OF HYSTERICA'S HENCHMEN.

BEEP

THE AMPOULE IS BELIEVED TO HAVE BEEN IMPLANTED CLOSE TO THE VAMPIRE'S HEART...
AND THE VILE ITSELF CONTAINS A CHEMICAL AGENT THAT WAS SYNTHESIZED FROM *CELLULOSE.*
WHEN MIXED WITH VAMPIRE BLOOD, A STRONG CHEMICAL REACTION OCCURS, WHICH RESULTS IN THE EXPLOSIONS WE'VE ALL WITNESSED.

SIMILAR TO "THE BLOOD OF AGNI"?
IT WAS CREATED IN THE MIDDLE AGES, WHEN THE ROYAL FAMILIES WERE FEUDING AMONGST ONE ANOTHER.
WHEN WARRIORS OR SPIES FELL INTO ENEMY HANDS, THEY WOULD BITE THROUGH THE TUBE, WHICH WOULD THEN CATCH FIRE.
IT WOULD CREATE AN EXPLOSION.
THAT'S RIGHT.
THUS THE VAMPIRE BECAME A BOMB.
OBVIOUSLY, THE EXPLOSION'S WE'VE WITNESSED ARE EVEN STRONGER NOW, DUE TO MODERN SCIENTIFIC ADVANCES.
AKIRA KNOWS FIRSTHAND HOW STRONG.
NUDGE

HYSTERICA'S PLAN IS CLEAR.
THERE'LL BE A FULL-SCALE ATTACK ON TOKYO.
SHE'S GOING TO SEND VAMPIRES WHO CAN PASS AS HUMANS TO DIFFERENT PARTS OF THE CITY, AND THEN BLOW THEM UP ALL AT ONCE.
IF SHE SUCCEEDS, IT WILL BE THE GREATEST SINGULAR ACT OF TERRORISM THIS COUNTRY HAS EVER SEEN.

THESE BOMBS ARE STRONG, BUT WE'RE NOT TALKING THE DESTRUCTION OF BUILD-INGS HERE.
MULTIPLE TARGETS COULDN'T DO THAT.
THAT MAY BE SO...
BUT WHEN THE INDIVIDUAL FORCES ARE COMBINED, THE RESULTING EXPLOSIONS WOULD BE DEVASTATING, NONETHELESS.
YES, THOSE ARE MY THOUGHTS AS WELL.
IF THEY SURROUND A TWENTY-METER AREA, EVERYTHING WITHIN IT WOULD BE COMPLETELY DEVASTATED.

MUTTER

TWO WORDS.
MASS TRANSPORTATION.

BUSES! TRAINS!
MOVING VEHICLES WITH NOWHERE TO ESCAPE.
AN ACCIDENT LIKE THAT WOULD PARALYZE THE ENTIRE TRAFFIC NETWORK OF TOKYO.

IT'S A TECHNIQUE OFTEN USED BY AL QAEDA, BUT ON A MUCH GRANDER SCALE.
HEH. I NEVER THOUGHT WE'D BE GETTING TIPS ON HOW TO KILL FROM HUMANS.

THE PLACE I BELIEVE THE ENEMY HAS THEIR SIGHTS ON THIS TIME IS THIS.
CLICK
THE SUBWAY.

I'M FAIRLY CERTAIN THEY'RE HIDING THERE DURING THE DAY.
AND IT'S OBVIOUS THAT THE SUBWAY WOULD POSE THE LEAST RISK TO THEM CONCERNING MOVEMENT AND PREPARATION.

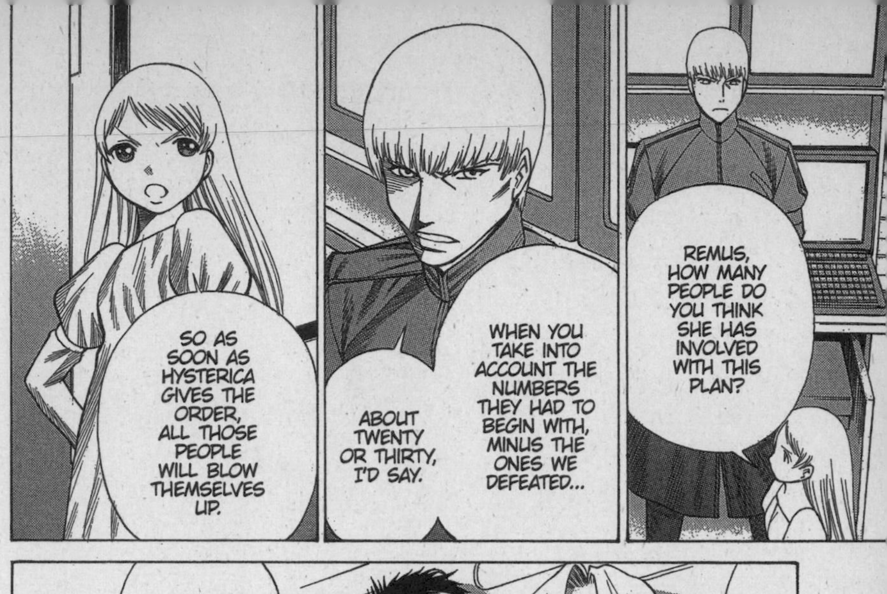
REMUS, HOW MANY PEOPLE DO YOU THINK SHE HAS INVOLVED WITH THIS PLAN?
WHEN YOU TAKE INTO ACCOUNT THE NUMBERS THEY HAD TO BEGIN WITH, MINUS THE ONES WE DEFEATED...
ABOUT TWENTY OR THIRTY, I'D SAY.
SO AS SOON AS HYSTERICA GIVES THE ORDER, ALL THOSE PEOPLE WILL BLOW THEMSELVES UP.

I CAN'T BELIEVE THIS...
PERHAPS WE CAN INTERRUPT THE TRANS-MISSION.
DO WE KNOW HOW SHE'LL BE ISSUING THE SIGNAL?

CELL PHONES ...
LAST NIGHT, SHE HAD ONE ON HER.
AND SHE USED IT JUST BEFORE THEY ALL BLEW.
BEEP
YES, OUR SCIENTISTS DISCOVERED THAT THE AMPOULE HAD A TINY CELL PHONE RECEIVER IMPLANTED WITHIN IT.
ONCE THE ACTIVATION CODE IS RECEIVED, IT TAKES ROUGHLY A MINUTE AND THIRTY SECONDS FOR THE FINAL EXPLOSION TO TRIGGER.

NOW THINK ABOUT IT, THERE ARE CELLULAR TOWERS EVERYWHERE.
AND THE RELAY TOWERS ARE CONNECTED TO THE ROOFS OF BUILDINGS, WHICH ARE ALL HOOKED UP TO POWER AND PHONE LINES.
TOKYO IS ONE GIGANTIC COMMUNICATIONS NETWORK, WHERE YOU CAN ALWAYS GET A CELL PHONE SIGNAL, NO MATTER WHERE YOU ARE.
EVEN... UNDERGROUND.
PIP
PIP
PIP
WHO ARE YOU CALLING, COUNCILOR?
CHIEF CABINET SECRETARY.

PLEASE GET THE PRIME MINISTER TO STOP ALL CELLULAR SIGNALS WITHIN THE CITY.
AND STOP ALL SUBWAY TRAFFIC AND SEAL THE UNDERGROUND ENTRANCES!
UH... IS THAT WISE?
WHAT?!
THE INSPECTOR'S RIGHT.
IF WE DON'T PLAY INTO THEIR PLAN, THEY'LL AMBUSH US.

AND ONCE HIDDEN, IT'LL BE DIFFICULT TO FIND THEM AGAIN.
DO YOU **REALLY** WANT TO CUT OFF THE CITIZENS FROM EACH OTHER?!
BEFORE WE ANNIHILATE THEM, SOCIETY WILL BE **PARALYZED!**
IF WE MOVE NOW, WE CAN CATCH THEM ALL AT ONCE!
IF THEY WANT A FULL-OUT WAR, **LET'S GIVE THEM ONE!!**
YOU...
YOU'RE GOING TO USE THE CITIZENS AS *BAIT?!*

NO.
I'M GOING TO BE THE BAIT!
THEIR GOAL IS TO CORRUPT SOCIETY AND CREATE CONFLICT BETWEEN THE JAPANESE GOVERNMENT AND THE BUND.
WELL, I'VE REALIZED SOME-THING...
I NEED TO KNOW MY WEAKNESSES IN ORDER TO SUCCEED.

THOSE WHO ARE GATHERED HERE...
ARE THE BEST HUNTERS IN THE WORLD.
OUR ENEMY HAS PROBABLY ALREADY PREPARED FOR EVERY POSSIBLE SCENARIO...
AND ARE JUST LOOKING FOR THE PERFECT TIME TO LAUNCH THEIR ATTACK.
BUT WE WON'T LET THEM PICK THE HOUR THIS TIME.
WE SHALL STRIKE FIRST!!

I'LL USE THEM TO MY ADVANTAGE AND TRAP THE ENEMY!
I'LL DRIVE HER AWAY BEFORE SHE CAN SEND THE ORDER, AND THEN THE VAMPIRE BOMBS CAN BE COMPLETELY ANNIHILATED!!
WHOA!
THAT'S RECK-LESS!
AND *HOW* ARE WE GOING TO FIND THEIR TARGETS IN THE CITY?
ROMU-LUS.
YES.
THE SEARCH IS ALREADY UNDER-WAY.

THREE-THOUSAND BEOWULF TROOPS UNDER LORD REGENDORF ARE SCATTERED ALL OVER THE CITY, SEARCHING.
WE OF THE EARTH CLAN WERE ORIGINALLY CREATED FOR HUNTING.
OUR HEARING IS FIFTEEN-THOUSAND TIMES BETTER THAN A HUMAN'S, AND OUR SENSE OF SMELL IS A HUNDRED-THOUSAND TIMES GREATER. WE CAN HEAR THEIR HEART-BEATS AND SMELL THEIR *SWEAT* UP TO A MILE AWAY.
AND IT'S EVEN BETTER WHEN UNDER-GROUND.

Panasonic
SO THIS IS A CHALLENGE.

I'M SURE THAT WOMAN IS WATCHING THIS.
SHE HAS TO BE. SHE'S PROBABLY GLOATING OVER IT RIGHT NOW.

YOU THINK THEY'LL COME, EVEN THOUGH THEY KNOW IT'S A TRAP?
DEFINITELY.

THAT'S JUST HOW VAMPIRES ARE.

SO HOW DID THINGS GO ON YOUR END?
WHAT DID YUZURU'S PARENTS SAY?

WHAT ...?
GRRR

SHE SAID SHE'LL LET ME TAKE CARE OF HIM!
SOMETHING ABOUT HOW STOCK PRICES ARE CHEAP RIGHT NOW, SO SHE DOESN'T HAVE THE *TIME*.

I'M SURE THEIR WORLD...

CONTAINED ONLY THE TWO OF THEM.

SHE KNOWS THAT THINGS CAN'T CONTINUE THIS WAY.
SHE'LL WORK IT OUT FOR THEM.
YOU'LL SEE.

WELL, I HAVE TO GO NOW.
SORRY TO SEND YOU ON SUCH A BORING ERRAND, YUKI.
NO, IT'S FINE. BE CAREFUL, OKAY?
YOU TOO. OH...DON'T TAKE THE SUBWAY!

ETERNITY IS LIKE THE NEVER-ENDING FLOW OF A GREAT RIVER.
IF YOU DON'T HAVE SOMETHING TO HOLD ONTO, IT'LL PULL YOU UNDER WITH ALL ITS SORROWS.
IF YOU DON'T...
HAVE SOMETHING TO HOLD ONTO...

HOW'S YOUR CUT? DOES IT STILL HURT?

N-NO, I'M FINE.
THAT'S GOOD TO HEAR. IT MIGHT STING, THOUGH, SO MAKE SURE TO LEAVE IT ALONE.

......
CAN I ASK YOU SOME-THING?
WHAT'S THAT?

HOW DID YOU BECOME A VAMPIRE, VERA-SAN?
WERE YOU ATTACKED BY ONE, LIKE ONEECHAN?
......
I OFFERED MY BLOOD TO THE PRINCESS'S MOTHER, THE PREVIOUS QUEEN, AND BECAME A VAMPIRE.
AND SO, I *CHOSE* AN INHUMAN LIFE.

WHY WOULD YOU DO THAT?!
WHY WOULD YOU *WANT* TO BE A VAMPIRE?

IT'S BECAUSE... I ADORED LUCRETIA-SAMA, THE PREVIOUS QUEEN.
I WANTED TO HELP HER, AND BE BY HER SIDE FOREVER. THAT'S ALL.

AHH... I'M SORRY...
NO, NO!

SADLY, IT WAS NOT TO LAST. LUCRETIA-SAMA PASSED AWAY, AND SHE ENTRUSTED HER DAUGHTER TO ME.
EVER SINCE THEN, HIME-SAMA HAS BEEN EVERYTHING TO ME.

"FOR GOD SO LOVED THE WORLD, THAT HE GAVE HIS ONLY BEGOTTEN SON."
HUH?

IT'S A VERSE FROM THE BIBLE. JOHN 3:16.

VAMPIRES ARE CREATURES WHO LIVE BY THEIR HEARTS.
YOU CAN LIVE FOREVER FROM JUST ONE FEELING, JUST ONE WORD.

JUST ...
ONE WORD...?

THIS IS TEAM ALPHA.
ON THE PLATFORM OF MARUNOUCHI LINE AT SHINJUKU STATION.
TWO MARKS.

THIS IS TEAM TANGO.
ONE MARK AT THE TICKET COUNTER, NAGATACHO STATION, HANZOMON LINE.
TEAM OMEGA. TWO MARKS AT TORANOMON STATION, GINZA LINE.
TEAM CHARLIE. THREE MARKS AT TOKYO STATION, MARUNOUCHI LINE.
TEAM ZEBRA. ONE MARK AT SAKURADAMON, YURAKUCHO LINE.
SO OUR SUSPICIONS HAVE PROVEN CORRECT. THE SUBWAY AND TRAIN SYSTEMS AROUND TOKYO ARE INDEED THEIR PRIMARY TARGET.

CHIYODA LINE, KASUMIGASEKI. THREE MARKS.
HANZOUMON LINE, OTEMACHI. CLEAR.
TOUZAI LINE, WASEDA. CLEAR.
REMEMBER, YOUR MARKS ARE LIMITED BY THE CELLULAR SIGNAL RANGE AROUND EACH STATION. THEY ARE AWAITING THEIR FINAL ORDERS FROM HYSTERICA...
ONCE RECEIVED, YOU WILL ONLY HAVE A *MINUTE AND A HALF* BEFORE THE BOMBS DETONATE.

BEOWULF SOLDIERS, PROCEED IN CONDUCTING A THOROUGH SWEEP OF THE SUBWAY AND SURROUNDING AREAS.
BUT DO NOT ENGAGE ANY HOSTILE ACTIVITIES.

WE MUST REFRAIN FROM ANY OVERT SHOWS OF FORCE UNTIL HER HIGHNESS HAS RENDERED HYSTERICA'S ORDERS INEFFECTIVE.
IF WE TIP OUR HAND TOO SOON, THE ENEMY IS LIKELY TO ACT PREMATURELY.
HOW DOES SHE PLAN...
TO SUPPRESS THAT SIGNAL?

SHINJUKU NS BUILDING
4:30 PM, SUNSET
YOUR HIGH-NESS ...
WE'VE CLOCKED TWO OBJECTS ON RADAR HEADED FROM TOKYO BAY TOWARDS YOUR AREA.
AT LAST.
WHOOSH

FLOOSH
FROOP
FROOP
FROOP
FROOP

FSHHHH
THANK YOU FOR COMING, MISS HYSTERICA.
MOTION
IT WAS AN INVITATION DIRECTLY FROM THE PRINCESS.
I JUST HAD TO SEE WHAT YOU HAVE TO OFFER ME.

FLASH
BUT TO TELL YOU THE TRUTH, I DON'T MUCH FEEL LIKE *PLAYING WITH* YOU TODAY!
YOU KNOW MY PLAN ALREADY, *DON'T YOU?*
WITH JUST ONE PUSH OF A BUTTON, THE TOKYO UNDERGROUND WILL BE *A SEA OF* ***BLOOD.***
THIS IS A GREAT COUNTRY, ISN'T IT? NO MATTER WHERE YOU GO, YOU CAN GET A GOOD SIGNAL ON YOUR PHONE.
DOWN IN THE LOWEST OF SUBWAYS, AND, WHY, EVEN ON THE HIGHEST OF ROOFTOPS!
OH WELL. I HAVE JUST **ONE** SIMPLE DEMAND.
I WANT YOU TO JOIN ME ON THAT HELICOPTER!!
THAT'S IT.
"TECH-NOLOGY WILL BE MAN'S DOWNFALL."
HEH. WHO SAID THAT AGAIN?

SO, MY DEAR PRINCESS ...
YOU DON'T WANT TO INVOLVE INNOCENT CITIZENS IN THIS SILLY LITTLE BUSINESS, NOW DO YOU?
I SEE...
THAT IS A SIMPLE REQUEST.
IT LOOKS LIKE THERE WOULD BE NO DANGER IN IT.
HOWEVER, THERE ARE ALWAYS UNFORESEEN SITUATIONS.
FOR EXAMPLE, WHAT IF THE HELICOPTER YOU RODE WERE TO--
KA
BLOOSH!!

WHA... ?
FRRRRRR
FWOOM
FWOOM
FWOOM
FSSHOOO

N...
NO...
TEMPER, TEMPER.
FINE!!
HAVE IT YOUR WAY!! YOU JUST SIGNED THIS CITY'S DEATH WISH!!!
WOULDN'T WANT TO GIVE AWAY THAT ACCENT, NOW WOULD WE?

YOU LITTLE BITCH!!
LOOK DOWN AT YOUR FEET, HYSTERICA!
!
NOW, VERA!!

CLICK
BAAAM
CRACK
CRUUUUUSH

FSH

We reconciled
and then we embraced.

And ever since then, we've been mortal enemies ——

VWOOOOSH
KICK

Chapter 18: Sacrifice

MINA-HIME !!!
FWOOSH
FWISH
FLAP
FOOM

CLINK
FWOOSH
SRRUUU

FLIP
THMP

FLICK
CRUNCH
YOU'VE UNDER-ESTIMATED ME, LITTLE GIRL!
INNOCENT PEOPLE ALL OVER TOKYO'S UNDER-GROUND ARE GOING TO DIE!!
AND IT WILL BE ALL *YOUR* FAULT, MINA-HIME!!
!

FSSSHHHH
WHAT ...
IS THAT?
IT LOOKS LIKE CONFETTI ...

CLOSE. THEY'RE SCRAPS OF *ALUMINUM FOIL*.
AND THEY'RE CREATING A DISTURBANCE IN THE RADIO WAVES IN THE AREA.
!

THIS SMALL AMOUNT WAS JUST TO CATCH YOU OFF GUARD.
THIS BUILDING HAS THIRTY STAIRWELLS. IT'S A GIANT BOX.
AND RIGHT NOW, THIS *BOX* IS FILLED TO THE BRIM WITH EVERY KIND OF ELECTRONIC JAMMING DEVICE KNOWN TO MAN.
NOTHING IS GETTING OUT OF HERE.
HYSTERICA...
YOUR PLAN'S FINISHED.

TIME TO HUNT!
GO, MY KNIGHTS !!
BEGIN THE MISSION!
GO!!
GO!!
SWF

TARGET A, ICHIGAYA.
CLEAR.
TORA-NOMON, CLEAR.
OTECHOU B. CLEAR.
ARRGH!

ANNIHI-
LATE
THEM.
NONE MUST BE ALLOWED TO ESCAPE! LEAVE NO SURVIVORS!!
GAME OVER, HYSTERICA. YOU LOSE.
ALL THIS BUILDING'S EXITS ARE BLOCKED.
THE ONLY WAY OUT IS...
KRO
OM!

I WON'T LET YOU GET AWAY, FRANCESCA.
SWISH
ARE YOU LISTENING, LITTLE PIGGY?!
YOU'RE NOT ALREADY DEAD, ARE YOU?!!
GULP...
HEH ...
YOU.

UNNH ...
AHH...
OH, LITTLE PIGGY! COME OUT ON THE ROOF!
SEND THE ORDERS WITH YOUR CELL PHONE!!
!
WHY ARE YOU LOOKING AT ME LIKE THAT?
THOUGHT I DIDN'T HAVE A BACK-UP PLAN?
IT NEVER MATTERED WHAT HAPPENED TO ME. ANY ONE OF THEM COULD'VE SENT OUT THEIR OWN DETONATION CODE.

GO, LITTLE PIGGY! DO AS YOU PROMISED!!
IF YOU DO, I'LL LET YOU GO! AND THEN YOU CAN BE WITH THAT LITTLE *BOY* FOREVER!!
YUZURU-CHAN...
YUZURU ...

NANAMI, *WAIT!!*

!
UGH!
FWISH

THWAM!
FROOO
HEH HEH HEH!
HIME-SAMA!
WELL, AT LEAST I KNOW THEY CAN SEND THEMSELVES THE CODE FOR CERTAIN NOW.
BRROOO!

I CAN'T LET SOMEONE AS WORTHLESS AS YOU STOP ME.
LUCKILY, I KNOW YOU CAN'T SURVIVE AN EXPLOSION FROM POINT BLANK RANGE.
AND WITH ANY LUCK, THERE'LL STILL BE A HEAD AND TORSO LEFT...
FOR ME TO CLAIM AND TAKE BACK HOME TO MOUNT... NOT THAT YOU'LL MIND!
SO JUST TRY TO MOVE!
YOU'LL FIND OUT FIRST HAND THAT THERE'S NO TIME LAG AT ALL WHEN THEY'RE THIS CLOSE.
HIME--!
KRRACK!

I'M THE ONE YOU WANT NOW...
VERATOS!!
BUT I'M NOT THE SAME PERSON I *USED* TO BE.
I'LL SHOW YOU THAT, ONCE AND FOR ALL!!

THIS IS TEAM ALPHA! TWO MARKS HAVE ESCAPED!!
REPEAT, TWO MARKS HAVE ESCAPED!!

HUFF...
PIP
PIP PIP
PIP
TMP
CODE:D
SELF-DESTRUCTION
TURN
WHAM

SWOOSH
CRUNCH
MARK B, CLEAR!
WHAT ABOUT THE OTHER ONE?!
AKIRA'S IN PURSUIT !!
SWF
投入口
TMP
WAIT ...!

HIKO ...?!
AKIRA!
KILL HIM!!
WAIT, HIKO!
WAIT !!
WHP

HUFF
HUFF
YUZURU ...
YUZURU-CHAN...
STAGGER

!

ONEE-CHAN...
I FINALLY FOUND YOU.

YUZURU-CHAN?
YUZURU-CHAN...?
YUZURU-CHAN!
I'VE BEEN LOOKING FOR YOU...
ALL ... THIS TIME.

COME WITH ME...
PLEASE...

LISTEN, YUZURU. I NEED A FAVOR FROM YOU.

IT'S IMPOSSIBLE TO DISOBEY A MASTER BY FORCE.
AND IT'S ALSO DIFFICULT FOR VAMPIRES TO FIGHT AGAINST THEIR DESIRES.
WHAT DO YOU THINK NANAMI'S DESIRE IS?
UH... ME...?

THAT'S RIGHT. IT'S NANAMI'S ATTACHMENT TO YOU.

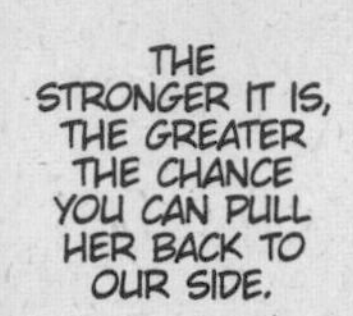
THE STRONGER IT IS, THE GREATER THE CHANCE YOU CAN PULL HER BACK TO OUR SIDE.

WE NEED YOU TO FILL THE GAP BETWEEN HER INSTINCTS AND CARRYING OUT HER MISSION!!
GULP...

ONEE-CHAN...
LET ME HELP YOU...
PLEASE?
AHH...
UH...

SWOOSH
SWISH!!
DON'T JUST STAND THERE!
AREN'T YOU GOING TO LEAVE?!
ONEECHAN!
LOOK AT ME!
YOU...
YOU NEED ME, DON'T YOU?!

I'LL BECOME YOURS, ONEECHAN!
SO COME AND STAY WITH ME!!!
AH...
AGHHH ...
HIC ...
I...

AHHH...
YUZURU-CHAN!
......
ONEE-CHAN...
I'M SORRY...

VRRRROOUUU
FSSHHH
WHOOOSHH
STOP!!
SHIT!
BAM
BAM
BAM
TOO SLOW!!
HIKO!
HIKO!!

K-CHA
K-CHA
K-CHA
K-CHA
K-CHA

GRRR
...
AHHH
...
THUMP
RIP
GRAAAAHHHHHH!!!

RUUUMBLE
LEAP
01 120

CRISH
OH MY GOD!!
EVERY-ONE, GET AS FAR BACK AS YOU CAN!!
DO IT NOW!!
TMP

KABU-RAGI-KUN...
HEH... YOU'RE PRETTY FAST, HIKO...
I DIDN'T MEAN TO SCARE YOU.
BUT IT'S OKAY NOW. DON'T WORRY.
I WON'T DO ANYTHING. JUST COME HERE, OKAY?

......
I CAN'T, KABURAGI-KUN.
IT'S TOO LATE.

YOU ASKED ME BEFORE, KABURAGI-KUN...
IF I KNEW WHAT IT MEANT TO BECOME A VAMPIRE.
I DIDN'T UNDER-STAND IT AT ALL.

NOTHING... NOTHING'S CHANGED. WEAK PEOPLE STAY WEAK.
THEY'RE TRAMPLED ON, USED, AND THEN JUST *THROWN AWAY.*
I CAN'T BEAR DOING THIS FOR-EVER...
I CAN'T TAKE IT ANY-MORE...

HOW DO YOU KNOW?
THE FUTURE IS AN OPEN BOOK! YOU CAN CHOOSE A NEW PATH!
I'M HERE! WE'LL FIGURE IT OUT TOGETHER!

I WISH...
I WISH I COULD HAVE TALKED TO YOU MORE.
IT'S NOT TOO LATE!!
YOU DON'T HAVE TO DO THIS, HIKO!!
AND THEN MAYBE...
THANKS...
AKIRA-KUN.

DON'T DO IT!!!
KA-BOOM

VRROOOOOOOR
KYAAAAAA!

SHAAA

ETERNITY...
IS LIKE THE NEVER-ENDING FLOW OF A GREAT RIVER.

IF YOU DON'T HAVE SOMETHING TO HOLD ONTO...

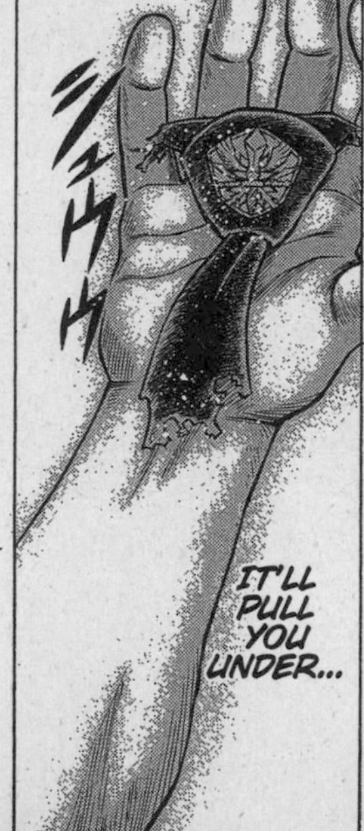

IT'LL PULL YOU UNDER...

SO HAVING THAT ONE THING TO HOLD ONTO...
MAKES ALL THE DIFFERENCE.
AGH...
UGH...

ARRRRRGGGGHHHHHHHHH!!!

KREEEH!
SWOOSH
THWAM

Chapter 19: Body and Mind

OH NO ...!
SHF
GRAB
WAY TO GO, VERA!
WHAM

VERA!
CRASH
BLUUP
KA-BOOM
POP
SSHAA
SHAA
RUUUMBLE
KREEE

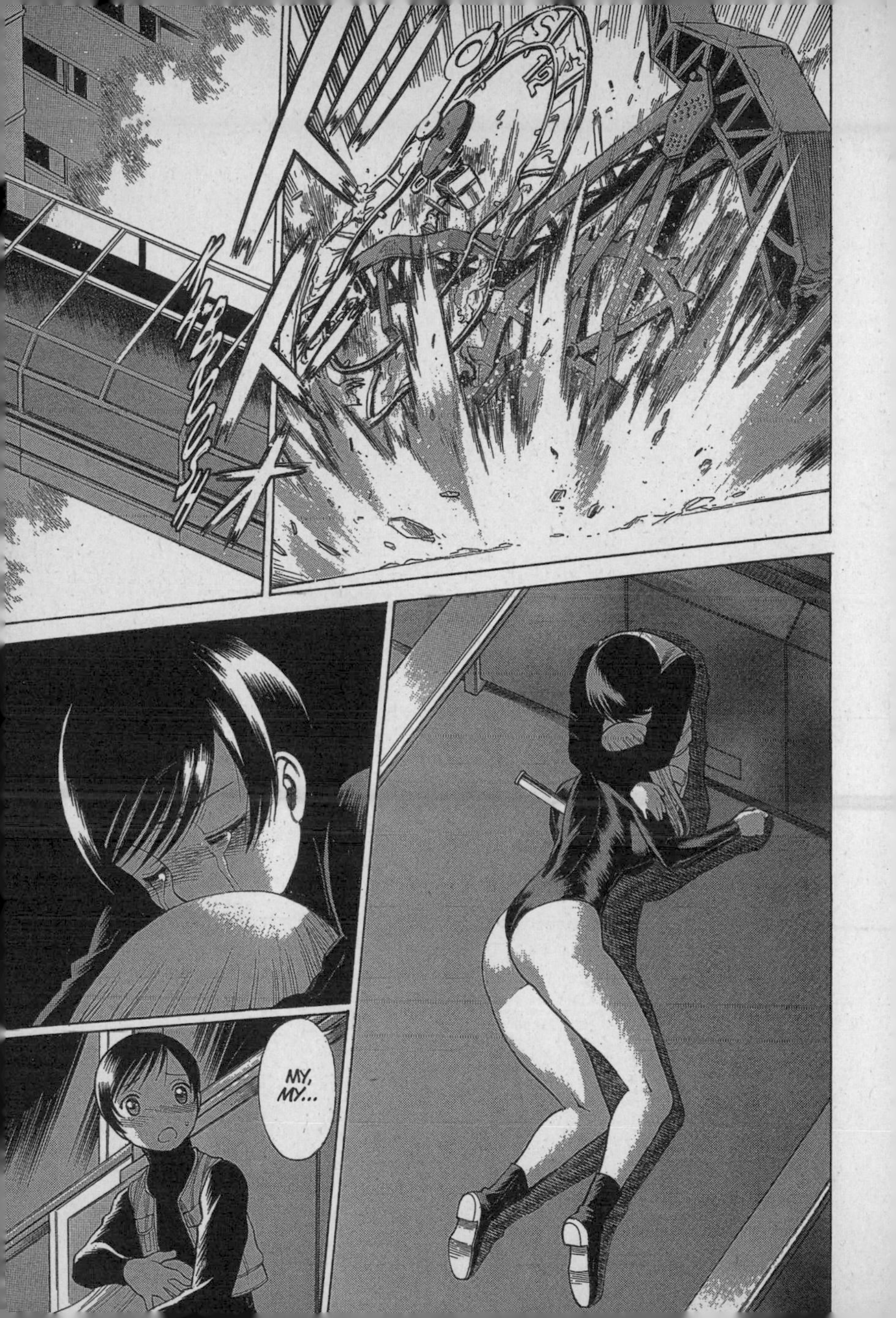
KRASSHH
MY, MY...

ISN'T THIS INTERESTING?
I GUESS THIS WAS THE END THAT AWAITED HER.
YES, I'M SURE SHE WOULD HAVE WANTED TO BE KILLED BY THE BOY SHE *LOVED.*
TMP
TMP
DON'T CRY, LITTLE PIGGY.
YOU'LL BOTH BE TOGETHER SOON ENOUGH.

SNATCH
UGH!
THE PAIN OF HAVING A LOVED ONE BETRAY YOU...
I'LL MAKE YOU FEEL IT TOO.
I WON'T LET YOU HAVE AN EASY DEATH, BOY.
HAAA
AHH!

SWOOP

WHAT ...?!

YOU...
WHO ARE YOU?!
...
NO... IT CAN'T BE...
MINA-HIME!!

HEH ...
SO THAT'S YOUR TRUE FORM!!
VERY WELL!
I WONDER WHAT MY MASTER WILL THINK WHEN HE HEARS THIS?!
HEH HEH HEH...
YOU'LL BE IN TROUBLE !!

DO YOU REALLY THINK I'D LET ANYONE GO AFTER THEY'VE SEEN THIS BODY?

TWITCH

HEH...
ARE YOU TALKING ABOUT THAT CORRUPTED BLOOD RELATION-SHIP?
I'M NOT ABOUT TO LET YOUR WISHES COME TRUE.
I'M GOING TO TAKE ADVANTAGE OF YOUR WEAKNESS.
!

FWIP
FWIP
GRAB
GRAB
CRACK
SHATTER

CRACKLE
CRACKLE
CRACKLE
KOOOSH
WELL, GO ON!
WE CAN'T HAVE THAT PRECIOUS LITTLE CHILD GOING SPLAT, NOW CAN WE?!
GAH!
AHH!!

OH, WELL DONE!
YOU'RE GOOD, PRINCESS.
YOU REALLY *ARE* A KIND PRINCESS IF YOU ARE SO SET ON SAVING A *HUMAN* CHILD.
HUH?
I CAN'T BELIEVE YOU.
DON'T YOU GET IT?
IF I PUNCH IN THE DETONATION CODE, BOTH HE AND YOU WILL BE BLOWN TO BITS.

WHAT'S WRONG? YOU'LL BE OKAY.
IT'S SIMPLE. DROP HIM... SO YOU CAN *KILL ME*.

CAN YOU DO IT?
OH, I SEE. YOU CAN'T, CAN YOU?
THAT'S YOUR WEAKNESS!!
AND BECAUSE YOU HAVE THAT WEAKNESS ...
YOU CAN NEVER BE MY MASTER!!
PLIP
DIALING...
0101212XXX XXX

AND SO I WIN...
PRIN-CESS.

IT'S ME!
CONNECT ME TO MASTER AT ONCE!!
I HAVE AN IMPORTANT SECRET ABOUT MINA-HIME THAT I'M SURE HE'LL LIKE TO HEAR!!
YES, MINA-HIME, NOW YOU'VE TRULY...

WHERE'S THE GIRL...?!
THRUST

ZAN
TWIST
TWIST
ZON
YOU'RE ...
YOU'RE ALIVE?
GYAAAAAA!!
I CAN'T...
BELIEVE IT.
HOW DARE YOU DISOBEY YOUR MASTER...?!
HER MASTER ISN'T YOU ANYMORE.
THAT STAKE WAS JUST LIKE THIS BUILDING. HOLLOW.
BUT IT WAS FILLED WITH A CULTURE FLUID CONTAINING DNA EXTRACTED FROM MYSELF.

OVER... WRITTEN ...
I STOLE HER FROM YOU.
NANAMI IS MY SERVANT NOW.

HYSTERICA, YOU SHOULD HAVE HAD NANAMI TAKE CARE OF ME FIRST.
BUT INSTEAD, YOU HURRIED TO TELL YOUR MASTER MY SECRET, LEAVING YOURSELF OPEN.

YOU SCREWED UP, HYSTERICA !!
I'VE WON!!
AGH...
NO...
GRAAAAAHHH!!
TMP

MINA-
HIME
!!!
VOOOM
FWOOSH
ZWSH
FWIP
PLOP

AND YOU THOUGHT YOUR OPPONENT WAS ME.
FRANC-ESCA.
SWOOSH
KA-THWACK!
FIZZLE

FWROOSH
AHH...
AGH...
UGH.
BLOOF
BLOOF
BLOOF
LIAR...
YOU SAID... WE'D BE TOGETHER... FOREVER...
FRAN...

WHOOOSH
RUMBLE
!
HIME-SAN.

FROOOOUR

VERA...?
FROOO

I'M THE ONE WHO TURNED FRANCESCA INTO A VAMPIRE.
SHE HAD LOST HER FAMILY TO THE SPANISH FLU AND WAS ON THE VERGE OF DEATH WHEN I FOUND HER.

......
IT'S OVER NOW.
IT'S ALL OVER.

YOUR HIGH-NESS...

NA-NAMI.
WILL YOU COME BACK WITH ME?
YES.
I'LL OBEY YOUR WISHES.

ONCE YOU ENTER THE BUND, YOU WON'T BE ABLE TO SEE YUZURU ANYMORE.
CAN YOU BEAR THAT?

......

AH, YUZURU.

......

VERA-SAN?
YES?

HAVE YOU EVER REGRETTED BECOMING A VAMPIRE?
NO.
NOT EVEN ONCE!

AH, THERE YOU ARE.
AKIRA, YOU'RE SAFE!
HOW'S KAICHOU?

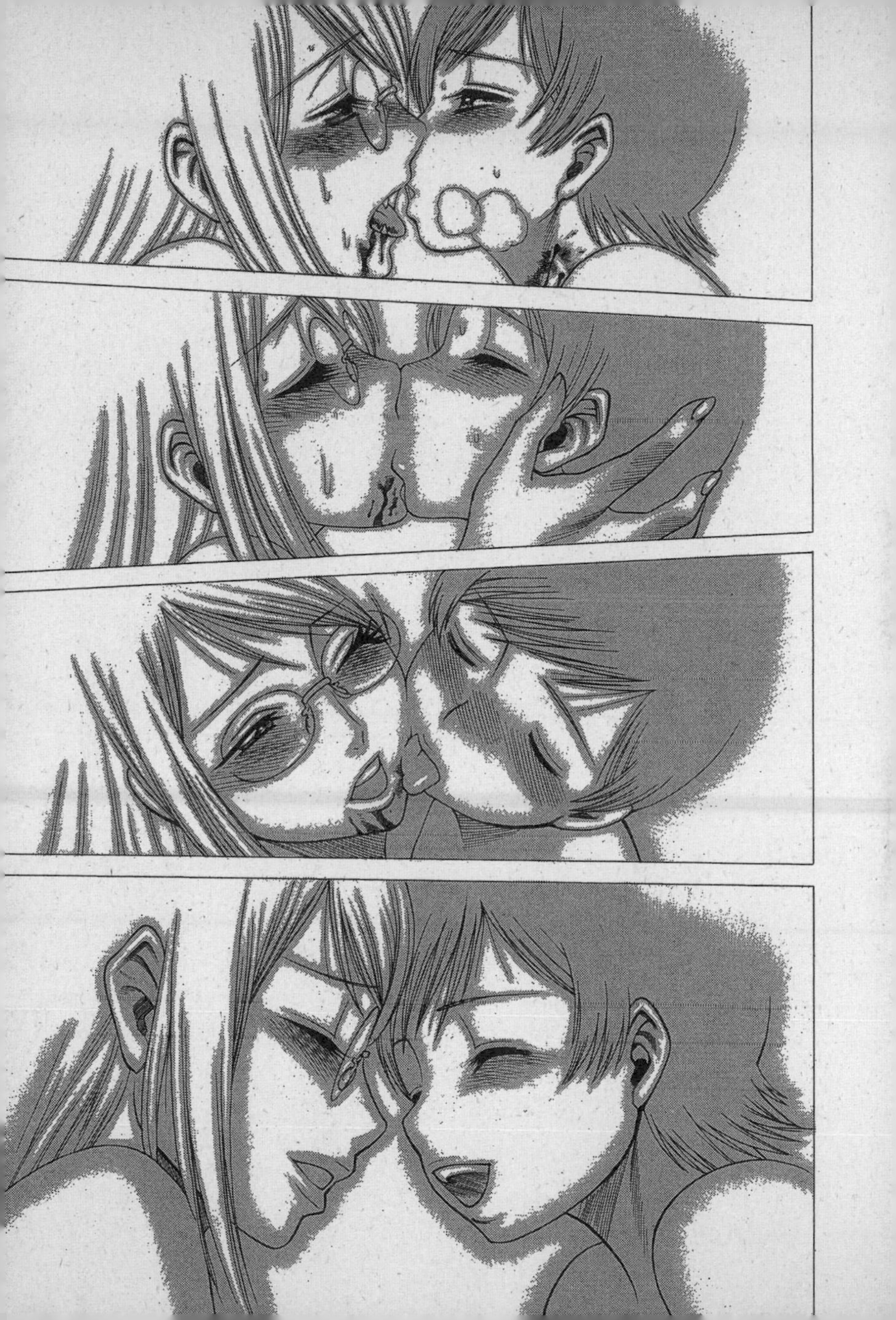

I SEE...
YOU WERE ABLE TO SAVE KAICHOU. THAT'S GOOD. THAT'S ONE, AT LEAST.

IT SUCKS, THOUGH...
I WISH I COULD'VE SAVED HIM...

....

BECOME STRONGER, AKIRA.
YOU DON'T HAVE TO DO EVERY-THING RIGHT NOW.
JUST TAKE YOUR TIME AND LET YOURSELF GROW.

FSSSHH

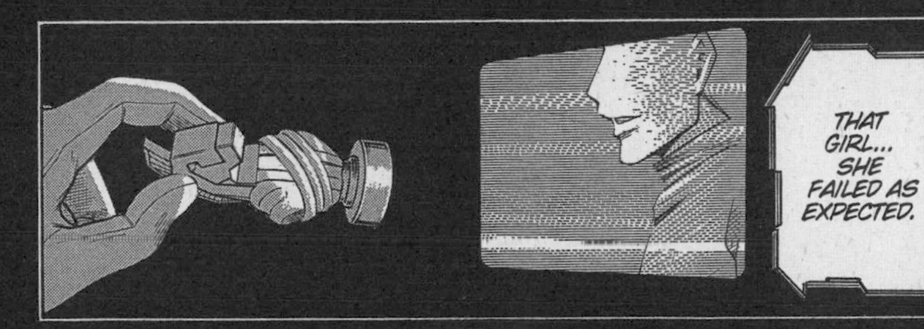
THAT GIRL... SHE FAILED AS EXPECTED.

I HAD NO EXPECTA-TIONS.
SHE WAS OF A HUMBLE BIRTH.

THAT'S NOT ALL.
CLACK
BEFORE SHE DIED, SHE GOT A HOLD OF SOMETHING. I DON'T KNOW WHAT, THOUGH.
COMRADES, IT'S A BIT EARLY...
BUT WHY DON'T WE GO AND CHECK IT OUT?

CONTINUED IN DANCE IN THE VAMPIRE BUND VOL. 4

STAFF
JUGGERNAUT
KOU HAYASHIKANE
TAKASHI KOMATSU
KENICHI NAKAMONO
SPECIAL THANKS
HIROSHI YAGUMO
KAORU SHINTANI

DANCE with the VAMPIRE MAID

EVER SINCE THEN, NERO AND NANAMI HAVE BEEN INSEPA-RABLE.

IT LOOKS LIKE YOU'VE TAKEN A LIKING TO NANAMI.
WELL, PRIN-CESS...

SHE HAS GLASSES AND HUGE BOOBS, AND SHE'S THE STUDENT COUNCIL PRESIDENT!

A TRIPLE THREAT !!
UH...
SOME-ONE BRING ME AN INTER-PRETER.

YOU'RE STILL GOING TO SCHOOL?
YES, HER HIGHNESS IS ALLOWING ME TO.

I'LL EVEN BE ABLE TO STAY STUDENT COUNCIL PRESIDENT!
SO I'M GOING TO DO MY BEST!

AT SCHOOL, SHE'S THE STUDENT COUNCIL PRESIDENT.
AFTER SCHOOL, SHE'S A MAID.
GLINT

PRINCESS, YOU UNDER-STAND... RIGHT?
HEE HEE HEE ♡
MAYBE YOU NEED A SHRINK MORE THAN AN INTER-PRETER.
Pervert.

ONEE-CHAN! ♡
YUZURU-CHAN!

UMM...
YOUR BROTHER?

MY BOY-FRIEND.
MY MASTER!

OH MY GOD!
HUH?
EH?

IT WOULD SEEM NERO'S A FAN OF SHOTA...
BUT THERE'S NO CONFLICT!
?

THEN READ THIS.

A DOUJIN?
WELL, I'LL JUST TAKE A PEEK...

GODS!!!
HMM, IT SEEMS THE SHOTA FANGIRL IS ALSO A POLY-THEIST.

THE NEW ONE JUST CAME!
THMP THMP
ALL RIGHT! LET ME SEE!

SO WHAT HAP-PENS NEXT?
I'M AT THE PART ABOUT VERA-SAMA.
WAIT, I HAVEN'T READ THAT PART YET!!

THIS IS SOOOO GOOD!
AHHHH!
THE PROTAG-ONIST IS SOOO SEXY!
OH YEAH!

AESTHETIC NOVELIST
SAEGUSA YUKI
PHEW!
SHE JUST GOT HER BIG BREAK AMONG ONE GROUP.
SHE JUST DOESN'T KNOW IT YET...

GIGGLE GIGGLE
SIGH

WHISPER WHISPER

AL-RIGHT!
WHAT IS IT THIS TIME?!
THE MODEL FOR THE PROTAGONIST OF THIS NOVEL WAS AKIRA...
AND IT WAS YAOI.
Ahhhh!
BLUSH

CONTINUED IN VOLUME 4!!!
You're so popular!
I'm so proud of you!
What has Yuki done?!

TRANSLATION NOTES

PAGE 29.2

Bosom friends - "Bosom friends" is the term used for best friends in Lucy Maud Montgomery's famous "Anne of Green Gables" series.

PAGE 30.2

Sasoi-uke - Yaoi term for a male character with feminine characteristics who "tempts" the more masculine character into a relationship.

Kyou-seme - Might be a reference to yaoi action between brothers or half-brothers (*kyoudai*), or to a character named Kyou who is the more masculine character of the pair.

CP - Yaoi term for a coupling or pairing.

Satou - Literally means "sugar."

PAGE 33.1

Fuzoku - A prostitution establishment. Many cater to specific sexual fetishes, such as Soapland (being washed), S&M and maids.

PAGE 135.3

Agni - The Vedic god of fire in the Hindu religion.

PAGE 151.1

While the Shinjuku NS Building may not be one of Tokyo's tallest buildings, the building's unique 30-story atrium running through the core of the skyscraper more than makes up for it. There is also a 29th sky-bridge that spans the atrium, an external glass elevator shaft, and the windows are covered in glass that catch the sunlight at different angles allowing the building to appear different colors.

On nous rèconcilia:Nous nous embrassâmes,et depuis ce temps-là nous sommes ennemis mortels.

On nous reconcilia:Nous nous embrassâmes,et depuis ce temps-là nous sommes ennemis mortels.

On nous réconcilia:Nous nous embrassâmes,et depuis ce temps-là nous sommes ennemis mortels.

On nous réconcilia:Nous nous embrassâmes,et depuis ce temps-là nous sommes ennemis mortels.

On nous réconcilia:Nous nous embrassâmes,et depuis ce temps-là nous sommes ennemis mortels.

On nous réconcilia:Nous nous embrassâmes,et depuis ce temps-là nous sommes ennemis mortels.

PAGE 154.4

"Technology will be man's downfall."
- In this context, this quote is likely a reference to Theodore Kaczynski's "Unabomber Manifesto."

PAGE 234.5.1

Shota - *"Shotacon"* is a Japanese sexual fetish term for when an adult woman is attracted to a young or underaged boy.

PAGE 236.3.6

Yaoi - Female-orientated fictional media centering on homosexual male relationships, oftentimes made by female creators.

story & art by Nozomu Tamaki

STAFF CREDITS

translation Andria Cheng
adaptation Janet Houck
retouch & lettering Roland Amago
cover design Nicky Lim
layout Bambi Eloriaga-Amago
copy editor Lori Smith
editor Adam Arnold

publisher Seven Seas Entertainment

DANCE IN THE VAMPIRE BUND VOL. 3

Visit us online at www.gomanga.com

ISBN: 978-1-934876-15-2

Printed in Canada

First printing: December 2008

10 9 8 7 6 5 4 3 2 1

YOU'RE READING THE WRONG WAY

This is the last page of
Dance in the Vampire Bund
Volume 3

This book reads from right to left, Japanese style. To read from the beginning, flip the book over to the other side, start with the top right panel, and take it from there.

If this is your first time reading manga, just follow the diagram. It may seem backwards at first, but you'll get used to it! Have fun!